Everyone's a Critic

Everyone's a Critic

⭐ ⭐ ⭐ ⭐ ⭐

Winning Customers in a Review-Driven World

Bill Tancer

Portfolio / Penguin

PORTFOLIO / PENGUIN
Published by the Penguin Group
Penguin Group (USA) LLC
375 Hudson Street
New York, New York 10014

USA | Canada | UK | Ireland | Australia | New Zealand | India | South Africa | China
penguin.com
A Penguin Random House Company

First published by Portfolio / Penguin, a member of Penguin Group (USA) LLC, 2014

Copyright © 2014 by William Tancer
ISBN 978 1 59184 638 3

Printed in the United States of America
10 9 8 7 6 5 4 3 2 1

Set in Garamond 3 LT Std
Designed by Elyse Strongin

In Loving Memory
Lori Minden Tancer
1968–2014

CONTENTS

Everyone's a Critic

1

★ ★ ★ ★ ★

The Review Revolution—
When Everything Is Reviewable

★ ★ ★ ★ ★

On Saturday, May 4, a reviewer by the name of "Mexico78" made an appointment to see "English Kim" at noon. The arrangement was simple: thirty minutes for eighty British pounds. Unfortunately the visit didn't go as planned. As Mexico78 recalled in his online review:

> I walked to the building. A bit chill & no jacket. Kim buzzed me in. She greeted me at the door & was shown into the room. Pricing discussed & cash exchanged. I was asked to get ready—which I did. Kim came back & gave me a £10 back as I'd accidentally over paid. What a lovely & honest gesture. Both ready we hoped onto the bed. I apologized about the cold hands & at that point my nose got moist. Kim jumps up, grabs her clothes, [she] says that she won't do snot. Before I could even dab my nose, my cash was on the bed and the front door was being unlocked. I was still undressed.

I don't have a cold. I am obviously embarrassed by my sudden moist nose. I'm clean, polite and I don't have any "special requirements". I've never been asked to leave anywhere. Excuse the pun, but nose very much out of joint.

In & out in less than 5 mins. With my cash back in my pocket. I wasn't rude. I didn't do anything on the naughty list. Rubbish really.

Recommended: NO

Would You Return: NO

Today everything is reviewable: this book that you're reading right now, what you had for lunch yesterday, the café that you frequent most mornings, your dry cleaner, your doctor, your dentist, your blender, your professor, your favorite music, your date (or escort if you're Mexico78), even you.

As the individual who calls himself Mexico78 walks down the street in a London suburb to meet a prostitute he's never met before, by researching her on Punterlink, a UK-based review site for escorts, he enters what could be a very compromising situation armed with online opinions from other johns (also known as punters in the UK). Before he leaves the safety of his hotel room, based on the postings of others, he knows what her flat looks like, whether it's clean, how safe the area is, her appearance, whether she's friendly, and the quality of her services.

Punterlink demonstrates why online reviews have become so valued by consumers; they provide information that allows parties to build some level of trust before entering a transaction. In the case of Mexico78, his pursuit of a London prostitute is fraught with risks, from contracting a sexually transmitted disease to getting arrested, robbed, or worse. As consumers continue to post their experiences and opinions online, the resulting trust built by the exchange of information facilitates more transactions.

Interestingly, according to Punterlink's stats page, johns are very positive reviewers. With a scale ranging from 60 (for the best) to 10 (for the worst), the average rating for all escorts on the site was 56.62. When geography is compared, ratings in eastern Europe were the most critical; Asian and American escorts were rated highest.

Punterlink is but one of thousands of examples of online review sites on every conceivable topic. The proliferation of review sites has largely been a huge boon to consumers, who benefit from access to more complete information about products or services.

Consumers aren't the only ones who can benefit from reviews. Businesses have the opportunity to get in front of their prospective customers at the point when they're making purchase decisions. For example, English Kim has a whole new channel to learn about and acquire new customers. By reviewing their online review history, she can quickly gather information on clients like Mexico78, such as what other prostitutes they've visited, and how they've rated them. She might also study her reviews in aggregate for consistent areas of complaints or compliments. She might even check out her rivals' reviews to discover if she's pricing her services competitively.

Given the opportunity to be in front of a prospective customer at the right place and time, you would expect that online reviews would be the number one priority on every marketer's list. Yet compared with traditional and online marketing channels, little attention is paid to this critical forum.

One possible explanation for this market inefficiency is that, as businesses, we've become myopic in our focus on social media, building out and updating our Facebook pages, broadcasting messages via Twitter, and posting images to Pinterest. An exhaustive number of conferences are held across the country in every conceivable industry to discuss the latest social strategies. While social media has undoubtedly changed the way most companies market, the social channel is best suited for building brand awareness. Very rarely does a social interaction such as a Facebook page like, or a tweet, lead directly to purchase activity. In fact, studies show that less than 1 percent of online transactions can be traced to links from social media sites.[1]

Another potential explanation for the lack of attention paid to online consumer opinions is that the online review ecosystem can be complex and noisy. While consumer narratives and star ratings increase the information flow between businesses and consumers, they don't necessarily provide perfect information. Online opinions, while providing means to increase trust between parties, can also contain inaccuracies, differing opinions, or omissions; in this case, English Kim's dislike for runny noses.

The importance of consumer opinions in consumers' decisions of what to buy continues to grow. According to a survey of U.S. consumers, close to 80 percent of the population consult online reviews before they make purchase decisions.[2] Despite the growing importance of online reviews to revenue, many business owners choose to ignore this channel, creating a massive market inefficiency. If business owners are willing to navigate the complexity of this space, that inefficiency can be converted to a significant gain.

60 Million People Can't Be Wrong

Just in case the opportunity to reach customers at the moment they're deciding to make a purchase doesn't appear real or important enough for you to leverage, consider how pervasive online review sites have become. In 2013, TripAdvisor ranked as the fourth most popular travel site in the United States of more than seventy-seven hundred sites, with 10.9 million visits per week. The site contains more than 60 million consumer-generated reviews.[3]

Yelp, a site that allows consumers to publish their own reviews on every conceivable category of business, including restaurants, dry cleaners, dentists, and car mechanics, just to name a few, had more than 9.9 million visits per week in 2013. According to Yelp, more than 27 million local business reviews have been authored by its army of consumer critics since its inception in 2004.

Since Amazon's launch in the late nineties, much of the company's success can be tied to the wealth of online opinions available to online shoppers. By hosting millions of consumer reviews, Amazon has become an indispensable resource for consumers from all walks of life.

In 2007, Yelp achieved the 1-million mark in online reviews posted on their site;[4] by 2013, that number grew to 54 million.[5] The dramatic increase in online reviews not only increases trust between buyers and sellers but businesses are also realizing that just having the presence of online reviews on their Web sites can dramatically increase revenue. Over the last several years, most e-commerce Web sites, selling anything from electronics to sporting goods to cosmetics, are hosting online reviews as a way of encouraging visitors to make a purchase.

According to research firm Reevoo, having ten to thirty reviews for a product online can increase conversions more than 3 percent. When a company has more than fifty reviews on a product, conversion rates can rise more than 4.6 percent.[6] For retailers that have tens of thousands of visitors per day, a 3 to 4.5 percent increase in transactions can have a major impact on revenue.

Here's the surprising fact: the reviews don't have to all be positive to increase conversions on a site. As we'll discuss later, in chapter 5, even bad reviews can be good for you. Reevoo found that 68 percent of consumers trust reviews more when they see both negative and positive reviews on a site, and when consumers purposefully seek negative reviews they are 67 percent more likely to make a purchase.[7] Given the substantial impact to their bottom line, national hotel and retail chains have ramped up their efforts to host consumer reviews on their sites. Bazaarvoice, one of the largest providers of third-party reviews, states that their user reviews generate 400 million page views per month. Still, some businesses are reluctant to feature reviews of their products on their Web sites, returning to a pre-Amazon misunderstanding that allowing consumers to post reviews online must be bad for business because negative reviews will discourage sales.

The influence of online reviews expands beyond Web site commerce. National retailers, such as the cosmetic chain Sephora, have launched mobile applications to help consumers consult online reviews while in their physical stores. In fact, in addition to its mobile app, online review terminals appear in many of Sephora's stores, where consumers can read cosmetic reviews supplied by other customers to help them make informed purchase decisions.

With the rising popularity of online review sites, the way that we make purchase decisions is evolving. While older generations might have relied exclusively on recommendations from friends and family when eliciting opinions on what to buy, younger generations are becoming more comfortable with relying solely on the popular opinions expressed on user-generated review sites. A 2012 study by Bazaarvoice indicated that baby boomers prefer friend and family recommendations (66 percent) to online reviews (34 percent), while millennials (those born between 1977 and 1995) prefer online reviews (51 percent) to the opinion of friends and family (49 percent).

When considering the long-term changes to recommendations, trust is increasingly shifting from friends and family to online reviews across all age groups. According to the findings of the 2012 Local Consumer Review Survey, among all age groups, 72 percent of consumers said that they trust online reviews as much as they do personal recommendations from friends and family. The study also found that 52 percent of survey respondents were more likely to visit a merchant if that business had positive reviews online. With each passing month, more and more consumers will look toward online reviews to make purchase decisions, and they'll have greater confidence that those reviews are fair and accurate.

Despite the ubiquity of reviews, if you talk with business owners about the impact of online consumer opinions on their businesses, you'll find that the majority believe that reviews probably don't affect their bottom line at all. Perhaps this is a defensive view triggered by business owners who have read their negative reviews.

According to research by restaurant industry firm That's Biz, 31 percent of restaurant owners feel that reviews on sites like Yelp, TripAdvisor, City Search, and Google are either mostly inaccurate or not accurate at all, while only 5 percent believe they are very accurate, and 24 percent believe they are mostly accurate.[8]

The most important question to pose is, do online reviews impact revenue?

To answer that question, at least from the perspective of restaurants, Michael Luca, an assistant professor at Harvard Business School, undertook a study to quantify just how impactful Yelp reviews were to restaurants. By analyzing the reviews of more than sixty thousand restaurants in Seattle and corresponding revenue data gathered from those same restaurants from the Washington State Department of Revenue, Luca was able to establish a causal connection between a restaurant's online Yelp rating and its revenue. His analysis demonstrated that every one-star increase in rating led to a 5 to 9 percent increase in revenue for independent restaurants.[9]

Another group of researchers, led by UC Berkeley assistant professor Michael Anderson, analyzed 148,000 Yelp reviews and reservation data from 328 restaurants gathered from an online restaurant reservation system. Their analysis found that a "half-star rating increase on Yelp translates to a 19% greater likelihood that a restaurant's seats will be full during peak dining times."[10]

With the upside of customer acquisition and increased bookings and revenue, you would think that businesses of all sizes would openly embrace the concept of consumer reviews.

The War for Customers

All businesses are engaged in a war to acquire customers. That war, however, has turned very bizarre with the advent of online reviews. Realizing the benefit that multiple five-star reviews can have on a business, common sense would dictate that every business would want to develop and deploy an online review strategy to maximize customer acquisition. Yet for many businesses, only the bare minimum is done: monitoring online review activity; if the business sells products online, then deploying a third-party review solution; and in some cases, responding to negative reviews. Even worse, some businesses ignore the space entirely, confused and angered by this new platform that provides their customers with a means to broadcast their experiences, both positive and negative, to every existing and future customer.

Like many other business owners, you might hate online reviews, but by picking up this book, you're taking the first step toward addressing the problem of review denial.

You should be happy, however, that you've taken the first step toward leveraging online reviews. What makes this scenario so compelling for your business is that you are a pioneer in a space where inattention creates inefficiencies among your competitive set.

First Step—Just Show Up

"Shoppers in the U.S. have over 2 billion conversations about brands per day."[11] If you're concerned that your online ratings are limited to the average number of stars you have, or the injustice of a negative comment, then you're missing the point. You need to be part of the conversation.

The advent of online review sites like Yelp, TripAdvisor, and the review components of eBay, Amazon, and other retailers has created a vehicle where you can easily converse with your customers, whether they've had a good or bad experience.

For the first time in business history, aggregate opinions of quality can trump brand, marketing, and advertising spend. A small start-up retail business, restaurant, hotel, or product manufacturer can vault above its competitors in customer acquisition simply by providing excellence. Conversely, businesses that thrived on the strength of their brand, or made up for poor service with big marketing budgets, are finding themselves in an increasingly uncompetitive position.

The consumer also wins in this scenario, particularly those who are more likely to be taken advantage of by unscrupulous business owners. Take a restaurant in a popular tourist destination like

Pier 39 in San Francisco. In a world before online reviews, a "tourist-trap" restaurant could prey on a potential customer's ignorance. If you were traveling and needed a restaurant, you probably chose one based on the recommendation of your hotel or, worse, solely based on proximity. Your choice was based on minimal, asynchronous information. On the other side of the equation, as the restaurant owner, you might rightfully believe that you'll never see most of your customers again. So why go to the expense of buying the best ingredients or spend time and money training the best staff when tomorrow there will be a whole new crop of potential diners swarming the wharf whom you can profit on while providing a subpar dining experience? Better to spend your money on advertising to attract tourists, placing costly ads in local tourist magazines or offering discounts through local hotels and motels.

As online consumer opinions become increasingly accepted, and more travelers check online reviews before making their trip plans, the tourist-trap restaurant will likely face extinction. As more granular detail is posted about every mediocre dining experience, the consumer will be in a position to make a true cost/benefit analysis when deciding to purchase a product or service. If I'm in San Francisco and find myself visiting Fisherman's Wharf, the average star rating on Yelp, TripAdvisor, or Open-Table will likely influence which restaurant door I walk through. For example, I would avoid Alcatraz Landing, which at the time of this writing ranks #3,135 of 4,840 restaurants, with an average TripAdvisor rating of one and a half of five possible stars. If you happen to be in my fair city, consider the advice of reviewer A.S.:

Probably the low-lite of our recent USA tour of three
cities.

We walked from our hotel down to the Landing looking
for a cafe, the obviously better ones were full so we car-
ried on and eventually hit the Alcatraz Pier where our
eyes lit up to see a cafe. Big disappointment, vast sums
charged for microwaved rubbish. Staff anything but polite. Served on paper plates, lacked taste. Not impressed.

It is almost as if they take the view of we have you here so
we'll have your money or you will go hungry. Amazing
that when you visit the island they wax lyrically about the
standards of food the inmates receive, clearly visitors are
rated (in the cafe only) lower than inmates were on the
Island.

As information becomes more synchronous, customers will
be won and lost by the experience sharing that online reviews
afford. Though most business owners don't share this utilitarian
view of online reviews, the by-product of this new flow of information is that businesses, in order to survive, must raise the
quality of their products and services or, alternatively, find new
ways to game the system.

If anyone can give me a sense of how online reviews are affecting local businesses, it would have to be my barber, Gloria. Not
only do reviews help drive business to her shop, All-Star Barbershop, but she also has several local business owners as clients.
I'm sure she's heard it all.

I visit All-Star Barbershop on Third Street in San Mateo every three to four weeks. On a late Tuesday afternoon I walk in to find Gloria sitting in the barber chair reading the paper. Gloria grew up in the business. Her dad is a barber, her uncles are barbers, and she doesn't hesitate to tell me about her family's business insight. "My dad told me to never lower my prices. Once you lower your prices you can't go back."

I ask her how business is. "Slow," she says, the same response I've gotten every month over the last two years, so I ask Gloria if she's heard of Yelp, not realizing that she has a "People love us on Yelp" sticker on the shop door. I mention that online reviews would be a great way to bring in some new business. By the look of her face in the mirror directly in front of me, I know I've touched a nerve and she tenses up. I consider the fact that Gloria is wielding a straight razor and wonder if this is the best time to bring up the topic of reviews.

"I had a guy in the shop the other day that gave me a one-star review," Gloria recounts as she returns to cutting my hair. "I know who that guy is, he wasn't very happy when he left, but you know what, he's lying." Gloria's All-Star Barbershop had a four-and-a-half-star rating with twenty-three reviews on Yelp at the time. Most of her clientele write five-star reviews for her shop, but occasionally she gets a negative review.

The haircutting business in San Mateo, a suburb of San Francisco, is mostly a referral and retention business. There are five barbershops in close proximity; their owners try to build up a loyal customer base and keep them with excellent service. With the advent of online reviews, their addressable market grew to any local Web surfer looking for a new place for a haircut. A strong overall rating can provide a steady stream of new customers, while a few negative reviews can bring business to a sudden halt. Understandably, the negative review Gloria is referring to, aside from referring to her as a "sheep shearer," is getting under her skin. Also a constant irritation is the fact that Gloria has seventy-three filtered reviews that are almost exclusively five-star reviews.

Beyond negative reviews, the most common complaint from business owners regarding Yelp's practices is that they use an algorithm to flag or filter reviews that are suspicious or likely to be fake. It's unlikely that many visitors read the filtered reviews on Yelp, as they appear at the bottom of a business's profile and require that you click through and verify your identity. Filtered reviews are also not counted in the average star rating that is so important to both the businesses and the consumers who follow reviews and make decisions based on them.

As we discuss the inequity of the consumer-review economy, Gloria's other customers chime in with their own review experiences, either as reviewers or as the reviewed. One waiting customer, a residential general contractor, comments on how reviews are being used as an outlet for his clients' aggression. He believes his business's profile has an unfair skew toward unhappy homeowners, and as a result, negative reviews are harming his business. Waiting third in line is an insurance salesman who comments on how much online reviews have changed his purchase behavior. He and his wife always check Yelp reviews before they try a new restaurant. Everyone else in the shop nods their heads in agreement. In this little barbershop, on a quiet suburban street, it's easy to see how influential reviews have become.

No matter how much Gloria and other business owners, large and small, despise consumer reviews, this online flow of information is experiencing explosive growth, and along with that there is an increasing importance in consumers' purchase decisions. According to Experian Marketing Services Data, the visits to TripAdvisor and Yelp from U.S. consumers has increased from 41 million visits per month in 2010 to more than 67 million visits per month in 2013, a growth of 63 percent.

Consumer reviews are also fueling a new redistribution of wealth. Those small business owners who have figured out how to harness the power of reviews find themselves with a flood of new customers, while those who choose to turn a blind eye to online consumer opinions, which in many cases includes larger, well-established businesses, are left wondering where their customers have gone.

Despite the overall negative sentiment that business owners might have regarding reviews, my goal is to show the Glorias of the world that not all is lost in this new space—and, in fact, there's much to be gained. Everyone, from the owner of a small business to the chief marketing officer of a large corporation, can benefit from online reviews and the asymmetric nature of online information.

In the chapters that follow, I hope to provide you with a thorough understanding of the constantly evolving ecosystem of consumer reviews, including the unique economics created by the review revolution, and the potential business gains you could experience from positive consumer-generated content.

The first step to understanding today's review-driven world is to appreciate the makeup and varying motivations of the millions of consumers who pen online reviews. Reviewers are as varied as the population, but we'll find that there are some specific demographics that are much more likely to pen reviews than the rest of the population. In chapter 3 we'll discuss how getting to know your customer reviewers and their needs are a necessary foundation to formulating a review plan.

Let's face it, the review world is fraught with problems, from extortion to fake reviews, excessive filtering, and questionable motivation. While all these issues might provide a justification for you to ignore what customers are saying about your business online, the fact that 80 percent of consumers are reading your reviews and trusting this imperfect channel before making a purchase decision should give you pause. Yes, there are shady reviews and a review "underworld." There's a good chance that a competitor has posted a fake positive review for his business, and a fake negative review of your business. Despite the imperfect nature of review sites, the fact that a majority of your customers check reviews before they enter your site or door is proof that this channel has become too critical to your business for you to ignore it any longer. In chapter 3, we'll conduct an exercise to desensitize you to your bad reviews and show you how even your most negative review can provide you with an advantage.

To build an online review strategy, let's start with a framework to help you focus on how to best position your business in your industry with these simple rules designed around the best practices of getting the most from your reviews:

1. Passion drives positive reviews.

2. Build power through transparency.

3. Make reviews central to the conversation.

4. Leverage reviews as motivation.

5. Give your customers something to write about.

These rules are good business practices that will help you to gather internal and external information, and to make decisions on how to best navigate your business toward success.

By applying the exercise in chapter 3 to the world outside the four walls of our own businesses, we'll be armed with the data necessary to make smarter, more effective changes.

While the world of online reviews has led to some bizarre outcomes, from comedic videos of actors reading humorous reviews to the overwhelmingly popular reviews of a banana slicer on Amazon, there is also a dark side to the consumer review space, with tales of bribery, extortion, even assault with a deadly weapon. This book will provide you with an action plan to deal with taking a proactive role when it comes to reviews, from joining the online conversation to knowing just when to respond to reviews.

Finally, we'll discuss how online opinions go well beyond today's traditional review sites. Due to the explosion of social networks such as Facebook, niche networks dedicated to specific interests, and 140-character opinions of your business broadcast on Twitter, dissemination of consumer reviews are exploding, and you'll need to know how to apply principles of review inventory beyond the traditional realm of online reviews. By building a foundation through a deeper understanding of the review eco-system, we'll explore how to embrace these channels in order to understand ourselves and our competition, and to find ways of increasing new business while retaining existing customers.

As I researched the material for this book, I discussed online reviews with a variety of individuals touched by consumer-generated content: numerous business owners, general managers of five-star hotels, the barista in my favorite café, waiters, hotel front-desk staff, manufacturers of products, and even authors who have felt the sting of a negative Amazon review. Just mentioning online reviews to the reviewed immediately brought a palpable tension to the conversation. Reasons for the negative reactions ranged from outrage over specific negative reviews that the business had received that weren't justified to complaints about the lack of process by which business owners could dispute a review posted by an online review site. There was also the ever-present concern that competitors were posting fake positive reviews on their own businesses as well as posting false negative reviews on their rivals.

If I were to sum up one of the chief concerns that businesses have about online reviews, it's the lack of control. There is a sense among most shop owners, specifically those in the hospitality industry (hotels, motels, restaurants, bars, cafés), that there is a strong causal link between their positive and negative reviews and the success or failure of their businesses. Based on the data that we will discuss in this book, their hunch may not be too far off.

2

Why Businesses Hate Reviews

★ ★ ★ ★ ★

To start my research for this book I talked with well over a hundred business owners. When I volunteered that I was writing about online reviews, there was a very common reaction. First, denial— "I don't pay attention to those sites"—then, almost immediately, that same person who didn't go to "those" sites started reciting their negative reviews verbatim. What I recognized in our conversations was that a form of cognitive dissonance was playing out.

Leon Festinger, the late social psychologist, developed the theory of cognitive dissonance, which describes the mental conflict we experience when we are faced with two disparate observations that can't both be true. In the case of online reviews, a business owner is faced with his belief that he is running a good business, while at the same time being confronted with online reviews that tell him his customers might have a different perception of whether his business is in fact good. Faced with this clear conflict, the owner decides that he is correct and, therefore, that the reviewers' opinions must be wrong. When most people are confronted with criticism of what they do, they want to re-solve the difference between what they believe are their best ef-forts and how the world perceives them. A lot of that criticism is driven by critics having a different perspective or opinion, some of it baseless, and some the result of an ulterior motive.

Given the amount of dissonance I heard during interviews, I wanted to start this chapter by addressing the elephant in the room. Consumer-generated reviews aren't perfect; they're far from it. What's worse is that business owners focus on those imperfections as attacks on their businesses. Despite their im-perfections, if we are to believe that reviews are important, we have to reconcile the thought that most reviews are honest and true even though they are critical and sometimes hurtful. Be-yond the cognitive dissonance, many of us have to come to terms with why we hate reviews.

Many business owners will attest that while most reviewers come to the experience with the altruistic goal of sharing their honest opinion on a meal, stay, or product purchase, there's a darker and at times bizarre side to the economy of consumer participation, on the part of both the reviewer and the business owner.

N. Gregory Mankiw, author of the bestselling textbook *Prin-ciples of Economics*, breaks down economics into ten essential prin-ciples. One of those seminal principles is that people respond to incentives, or that an individual's behavior changes when costs or benefits change. In the case of consumer reviews, business owners realizing the benefit of online reviews might be incentiv-ized to write positive faux reviews of their business or negative reviews of a competitor. They may even pay complete strangers who have never visited their establishment to write a review. A visit to any city's Craigslist's online classifieds will yield listings such as the following:

> Yelp Reviews: looking for any Yelpers in good standing account to post reviews on businesses, if interested please provide a name phone number ant a link to your Yelp account. $ 25.00 a review

Bizarre behavior isn't limited to consumer reviewers. In 2009, Diane Goodman, the proprietor of the now closed Ocean Avenue Bookstore in San Francisco, California, was incensed by Yelp reviewer Sean C.'s comment that her store "is a TOTAL mess." Goodman began sending Sean threatening e-mails via his Yelp account, and the encounter between them culminated with Goodman tracking down Sean C. at home and forcing her way in. Sean called the police, and Goodman was arrested and transported to San Francisco General Hospital for psychiatric evaluation. When interviewed by *Inc.* magazine for its story on Yelp, she stated, "I've never met any store owners that liked Yelp. We're all gritting our teeth. It's evil."[1]

Given the challenges of review gamesmanship at best and criminal activity at worst, many business owners have decided to ignore online reviews entirely. Others, though, have found their own way of protesting what they feel are uninformed or unjust reviews.

Extortion

Michael Bauer, food critic for the *San Francisco Chronicle*, reports that he has received several e-mails from restaurant owners detailing extortion attempts on behalf of online reviewers. Marsha McBride, owner of Café Rouge in Berkeley, California, e-mailed Bauer:

> Customers have begun threatening to "Yelp" the restaurant if their demands are not met. Cafe Rouge experienced this phenomenon twice within the past month when comps were demanded with the threat that a harsh review would follow on the Yelp website if we didn't comply. The expectation of how much to comp is also at issue, where a glass of wine, an appetizer or dessert no longer suffices.

Claims of reviewer extortion are quite common in the restaurant industry. Sonny Mayurga, owner of the Red Rabbit Kitchen and Bar in Sacramento, California, learned firsthand about the power of the consumer in a review-driven world. His restaurant has more than 300 reviews and a solid four stars on Yelp, four stars on Google reviews, and 188 reviews and four and a half stars on Urbanspoon. As they are for many restaurants, online reviews are an important marketing channel for attracting new diners to Sonny's establishment. Given what was at stake, you could understand why the call from a guest who had dined at the restaurant the previous night felt like an attempt at extortion. The caller claimed that he and his party had gotten food poisoning from their meal at the Red Rabbit. Since Mayurga had no way of proving or disproving the caller's claim, he offered him a sixty-dollar gift certificate to a restaurant of his choice. The man said that he deserved one hundred dollars for his trouble, and if the restaurant refused to pay he would write a bad review on Yelp and report the restaurant to health authorities.

Combing through the complaints received by the Federal Trade Commission,[2] there are numerous allegations of extortion:

> I work as a receptionist at an Italian Restaurant and yelp elite member [NAME REMOVED], asked me to contact my manager to ask if in exchange for FREE dinner and drinks, he would write a glowing review. He said he does this all the time, that this is common practice for him. This is totally wrong. This is not what an elite member of yelp should be doing. Additional Comments: Please take this guys badge away or close his account. I was scared that he was going to write a bad review when I told him no way would I comp him a free meal and ask my manager.

Prior to the advent of online reviews, it wouldn't be uncommon for a business owner to encounter a dissatisfied customer who might, at worst, tell his friends and family not to frequent an establishment for bad food or service. Today's disgruntled customer has the online equivalent of a bullhorn, capable of broadcasting discontent to countless review site visitors who might be considering trying out a new restaurant.

Just the mention of online review sites to a business owner

can evoke strong emotions that could be described as visceral: spines stiffen, faces contort, eyes narrow. Chefs often have the worst reactions.

When asked about their online reviews, business owners, who all stand to gain from review sites, usually respond by recalling a negative review, perhaps published online by a dissatisfied customer or a competitor, or perhaps merely the perception that some reviews were authored by a competing business in the same neighborhood.

Restaurant owners responding to the That's Biz survey about online reviews felt that one of the most frustrating things about reviews is the small sample of reviewers versus all customers. Making matters worse, many business owners believe that those customers who have had a poor experience are more likely to write a review than satisfied customers. Many owners also feel that ex-employees and unruly customers write many of their negative reviews.[3]

In some cases, online reviewers seek to exercise their newfound powers in much subtler ways. Big Gay Ice Cream in New York's Greenwich Village had a run-in with an Elite Yelper about store hours. The owners received an e-mail from the Yelper, who wanted to arrange a tasting at the ice cream shop before they opened their doors to the general public. The Yelper also requested that the store provide a tasting of every ice cream that they serve along with a special flavor developed just for them. The e-mail alluded to the potential positive reviews, stating, "just think of all the great reviews you're going to get."

Conflict of Interest

Beyond extortion and negative reviews, the next most common complaint I've heard from businesses is that there's a conflict of interest. In the case of Yelp, their primary source of revenue is online advertising, which appears in the form of paid listings at the top of user-generated reviews. The complaints arise from the fact that Yelp's sales force sells advertising to the same businesses that are reviewed by consumers. Many business owners have claimed that Yelp's sales team has implied that they would, and in some cases outright threatened to, use the filtering technology to lift negative reviews and remove positive reviews if a business won't buy their paid advertising.[4]

OpenTable, a restaurant reservation site, has been accused of a different form of conflict of interest—deleting reviews that were damaging to their restaurant-clients. Over the years several start-ups in the review sector have tried to build their businesses on verified reviews, but few have survived. OpenTable is an example of a verified review system (albeit their core business model isn't the review but the reservation that at times is driven by a review). When making a reservation on OpenTable, you receive an e-mail requesting that you review the restaurant. The only individuals who are capable of writing reviews on the site are those who have completed their reservations (or are verified diners of the restaurant). By creating this closed-loop review system, OpenTable can eliminate the problem posed by phony reviews.

Even closed systems have challenges. In the spring of 2013, a diner wrote to Michael Bauer to complain about a review she had written that she wasn't able to post to OpenTable. The diner had visited a San Francisco landmark restaurant in the city's theater district and was disturbed by the presence of live and dead flies inside the dining room. The diner decided to respond to OpenTable's request for a review by posting her experience. After hitting the submit button to post her review, she received a message back from OpenTable informing her that her review violated their policies. According to Ann Shepherd, senior vice president for marketing at OpenTable, reviews have to be credible to be valued by other consumers and restaurants, and that's the primary focus of deciding which reviews OpenTable's review board decides to remove from their system. According to Shepherd, "It's really easy for diners to make comments that can be very damaging to a business." The allegation of flies in the restaurant, which alludes to a possible health-code violation, was removed because of the potential harm it might cause the restaurant.

Filtering

Yelp has been the subject of more than 650 complaints filed with the Federal Trade Commission. By reviewing these complaints, it becomes evident that many business owners believe that review sites filter out negative reviews and promote positive reviews for businesses that advertise on their site. One complaint released with a Freedom of Information Act request from a restaurant owner in Los Angeles alleges:

what yelp does is that they prey on restaurants with bad bogus reviews I think they have a team that writes bad reviews for restaurants and after a couple months later they have a yelp sales rep call so you can join their membership $300 when i joined most of the bad comments were gone about my restaurant but I dont think it's fair practice if you dont pay for the membership you dont have a chance to rebuttal the comments. I am very afraid of this company because they have the power to make any restaurant go out of business.[5]

Yet another business in Denver, Colorado, alleges:

This company contacted me about reviews of my business on their website. They said they could "help me improve my rating" if I were to spend $350 a month in advertising. Since they are not the ones writing reviews, there is no way they could make this happen, unless they were to filter the bad reviews. I feel like I am being blackmailed.[6]

Yelp has vehemently denied that its filtering technology has any relationship to its advertising sales initiatives, and has won two legal challenges from this claim. Still, allegations that Yelp is extorting ad sales protection money from small businesses continue.

Michael Luca, the Harvard professor who analyzed the effect that Yelp reviews have on restaurant revenue, addressed the question of fraudulent reviews and whether the Yelp filtering algorithm favors their advertisers. In his research, Luca estimated that 13 percent of restaurants' reviews are "fake," or written by someone other than a business's customer commenting on their experience. This large percentage of fake reviews sets up the need for a robust filtering algorithm.[7]

If the slew of FTC complaints are valid, that is, that Yelp selectively filters out bad reviews for advertisers while promoting (or unfiltering) positive reviews for those same advertisers, then there should be a difference in the breakdown of filtered reviews by advertiser and nonadvertiser.

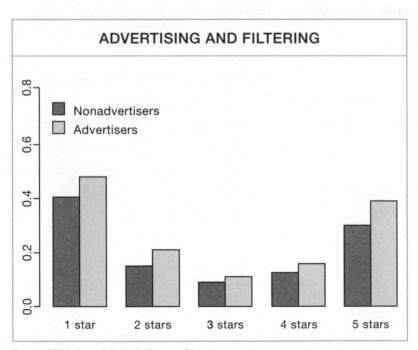

Source: HBS; Luca, Michael; Zervas, Giorgos

If there were a positive bias toward advertisers, we would expect the distribution of their reviews to skew toward four and five stars in the above chart. Likewise, we would expect non-advertisers to skew toward lower-starred reviews on the left. In this graph, however, the distribution of star ratings is essentially the same for both groups.

To date, no court has ruled in favor of plaintiffs asserting that Yelp filters based on the decision to advertise with the site, and no data that corroborates this claim has been offered. Despite Yelp's success in the courtroom, many small businesses persist in claiming that salespeople associated with the site have hinted that advertising with Yelp will help filter out negative ads and push up positive ads. Yelp continues to deny that claim.

Regardless of Yelp's claims and the data provided by Luca, the power to use Yelp reviews as a tool to extort businesses is documented. That power could be wielded by a review site, consumers writing reviews, or an outside influence like Andrew J., a former salesperson at daily deal site Groupon. In August 2013, Andrew was trying to sell the San Francisco restaurant Sauce on using his company's site to drive more business to the restaurant. When Sauce's owner hung up on him, the salesman retaliated by sending a threatening e-mail to him:

> As a resident of San Francisco for over 25 years, I have a huge network of friends (ages 25–40) that all are extremely active on Yelp as well as other social media. I will gladly let them know how you treated me as well as my feelings about the people who run Sauce.[8]

Sham Reviews

The Harvard study showed that consumer reviews can have a substantial impact on revenue, between 5 and 9 percent per star for restaurants.[9] With so much at stake, why don't businesses write up some phony five-star reviews themselves? The simple answer is that some do.[10]

Perhaps the promise of more room bookings is what drove Peter Hook, director of communications for Accor hotels, to post more than one hundred phony reviews for his company's hotels, along with negative reviews for competitive properties, on TripAdvisor.[11] Mr. Hook isn't alone in his guerrilla tactics. In 2009, T. Carpenter, communications manager for higher-end coffeemaker De'Longhi, decided to post glowing reviews for several machines in the coffeemaker's product line. In response to a complaint by a *Wall Street Journal* journalist, De'Longhi responded by saying:

> We find no false statements in any of the reviews posted
> by T. Carpenter. Our employees are passionate about the
> products we make and sell and this is a quality we are
> quite proud of in all our associates.[12]

The folks at De'Longhi see nothing wrong with their employee writing shill reviews for their products. Hook and Carpenter were communications managers at their respective companies. Could it be that these individuals didn't see the ethical issue with posting phony reviews, or was being so close to the product and invested in its success just too attractive for them to care about ethics?

Most business owners are smart enough to know not to write

fake reviews for their own businesses, but, unbeknownst to most travelers, that hotel review you're reading might have been penned by a hotel manager on the other side of the globe, thanks to tripadvisor-reviewers.com.

Hotel Owners Combat TripAdvisor on Their Terms

Some enterprising business owners and managers in the hotel industry have forsaken the paid-for review and opted for creating a review co-op to trade reviews among themselves. Discovered through a Google search, tripadvisor-reviewers.com, with the tagline "owners posting reviews for owners," is blatant in its mission to create a community where reviews can be traded within the hospitality industry. The consortium was founded by a group of nine anonymous hotel owners in the United States, Europe, and New Zealand. In the "how it works" section of the site, the community owners tout the method that they have created to thwart detection by TripAdvisor:

> Write your own reviews and have them validated (if needed) by other members from other countries OR you can ask other members to write (a) review(s) on your behalf, knowing they are using clean IP's from the country the reviews originate from.[13]

The site, along with providing a means to exchange reviews, also sells anti-TripAdvisor baseball jerseys emblazoned with slogans like "TripAdvisor Liars" and "STOP TripAdvisor." They also offer review ghostwriting services for twenty dollars per review. According to the site, 100 percent of all proceeds from paid reviews go to a charity to help abused and neglected animals (although the site doesn't specify which charity).

I believe that the existence of these shady practices has been the catalyst for some business owners to decide to ignore online reviews completely. Dismayed by the number of questionable five-star reviews for a competitor and negative reviews of their own business, some feel that natural selection will eventually weed out these unscrupulous businesses.

While most business owners are presumably smart enough to avoid the pitfalls of writing their own reviews, they're also aware that a handful of five-star self-reviews are not enough to make a difference. Instead they seek the assistance of reputation management companies or "task-based" marketplaces such as Amazon's Mechanical Turk, Odesk, or Fiverr. These marketplaces link business owners with individuals who typically work on short, low-cost repetitive tasks such as translating Web pages, conducting market research interviews, or writing fictitious online reviews.

In a typical posting on the site Fiverr, user Rezafive offers to:

> Post 2 Negative Google Reviews about your online services or products or competitive business using US verified accounts. I will submit the review from different IPs. I will use 2 different username to submit these reviews. You can also supply the reviews as you know better than me about your competitor

Rezafive has a 100 percent satisfaction rating, and there are hundreds like her ready to review a business for only five dollars per review.

In January 2009, Belkin's president, Mark Reynoso, posted a public apology to its corporate Web site regarding one employee's overzealous attempt to garner positive reviews for a four-port USB hub.[14] Reynoso's apology was prompted by an Amazon Mechanical Turk request that blogger Arlen Parsa stumbled upon as he browsed postings for transcription work.[15]

In the Mechanical Turk posting, the Belkin business development manager requested the following for sixty-five cents per post:

- 100% rating (as high as possible)

- Between 25 and 50 words

- Write as if you own the product

- Tell a story of why you bought it and how you are using it

- Thank the website for making you such a great deal

- Mark any other negative reviews as "not helpful"

The request then provided further instructions and a link to the specific product. After the blogger's post made the rounds at Digg, CNET, Engadget, and other sites, the company president had no recourse but to publicly apologize and work with Amazon to have all the fraudulent reviews removed.

Some freelance reviewers have harnessed their entrepreneurial spirit to create "reputation management" businesses to profit from providing reviews for a few in a more systematic, scalable way. In 2012, U.S. firms were expected to spend more than $700 million dollars on technology to monitor online opinions, and according to research firm BIA/Kelsey, that number was expected to double in 2013.[16]

While there are many legitimate reputation management companies, over the last few years, as the popularity of online reviews has blossomed, a number of shadier outfits offer fake reviews in every business category.

In 2012, a *New York Times* article shed light on the review-for-hire industry when it profiled Todd Rutherford's now defunct site, gettingbookreviews.com. Catering to the literary community, Rutherford and his army of independent contractors would write twenty reviews for just shy of one thousand dollars.[17]

Other companies, going under the moniker of "online reputation management," seek to get negative reviews removed, even those that are valid, through a variety of tactics. Profile Defenders claimed in its press release launching the business that it would provide a 100 percent guarantee of removing unwanted Yelp reviews for a fee starting at five thousand dollars.[18] On its site, the company lists the sources for negative reviews, including disgruntled ex-employees, unreasonable customers, and your competition. While Profile Defenders doesn't detail exactly how they're able to remove all negative reviews, its frequently-asked-questions page lists clues such as "preparing necessary paperwork to prove content as libelous or slanderous" to threatening legal action to convincing posters to remove their negative reviews.

Bribery

Back in Gloria's All-Star Barbershop, Gloria shares a personal experience of reviews gone bad. That prior week, she decided to find a new hair salon to get her own hair colored. After doing research on Yelp she found one that had an almost perfect five-star rating. She called and immediately sensed that something wasn't right. The employee answering the phone at the salon didn't sound that professional and had trouble making an appointment for her. Deciding to disregard her intuition, Gloria went on the appointed date and time to her new salon to get a color treatment. Once guided over to her stylist's station by the receptionist, she waited for her stylist to return. That's when she overheard the conversation in the station next door. "I don't understand why you're not giving me twenty percent off this treatment like you did last time," the customer said. "No, you don't understand," the stylist replied, "you only get the twenty percent when you bring in a copy of your five-star Yelp review, but that's only a one-time discount." Now it all made sense to Gloria. If the five-star reviews were all the product of a discount/bribe to customers, that would also explain her underwhelmed impression of the shop. She got up and quickly left the salon.

Not all attempts to get positive reviews are as malevolent as the salon example. While a common practice of asking for reviews on hotel and restaurant checks seems reasonable, there is a much higher likelihood of businesses incentivizing positive reviews if they offer discounts for reviews. In San Francisco in 2009, for example, a local restaurant chain called Mel's Drive-In decided to engage in a little social marketing themselves. Taking the cue from Hotmail and their viral campaign via e-mail signature, Mel's Drive-In decided to use the customer check as the next best means of encouraging reviews and increasing revenue. On the bottom of the diner's check was a printed offer: "Want 20% off? Go to Yelp and write a review. Bring it in with this coupon and receive a 20% discount! That's a great deal."[19] While policies at most online review sites discourage the practice of offering incentives for reviews, the practice might actually yield more useful reviews and increased guest engagement.

University of Pittsburgh assistant professor Andrew Stephen conducted an experiment in which he asked two groups of people to play a fun video game, then asked them to review that game afterward. One group was given a one-dollar incentive to write their reviews, while the second group was not given any compensation. After the reviews were written, people who hadn't played the game were asked to rate the usefulness of each review. The reviews of those who were paid one dollar were judged to be more useful overall than the reviews of the non-incentivized group. Those who judged the reviews were more likely to want to play the game after reading the more helpful reviews.[20] Based on this experiment we could conclude that Mel's practice of incentivizing reviews with a future discount could result in more useful reviews that could draw more diners.

While Mel's example is relatively benign in its implementation, other businesses have tested the limits by offering discounts with proof of a positive review.

The practice of fraudulent reviews intensifies when it comes to reviewers with more influence—programs like Yelp's Elite and TripAdvisor's Top Contributors. What is often referred to as "pulling the Elite card" refers to the subtle practice of letting a restaurant or business owner know that you have Elite status and that their business would benefit if they provided preferential treatment. Review sites have become savvy to this practice of bribing or paying for positive reviews, and take action, from removing the offending review to posting a warning to consumers on the business's page that some reviews were obtained fraudulently.

Yelp and TripAdvisor Fight Back

Actions to subvert the collective opinion in the business owner's favor are fraught with problems.

First, in today's climate, consumers are becoming more cynical, and in that cynicism they have assumed the role of policing online reviews, looking for phony postings by business owners. At a minimum, it seems that consumers are becoming critical when reading reviews and factoring questionable entries when making a purchase decision.

Second, review sites themselves see phony online reviews as one of the biggest threats to their business, and they're fighting back any way they can.

In the fall of 2012, Yelp launched a sting program to ferret out and shame businesses that post phony reviews or hire others to post on their behalf. To carry out the sting operation, a Yelp employee posed as an Elite Yelper online to discover businesses that were willing to pay for phony reviews. In their initial effort they identified eight businesses that were engaging in pay-for-review practices. In one case, the undercover employee was offered two hundred dollars from a jewelry store in San Diego to write a phony review about a custom-designed ring.[21] Rather than delete the business's account from the service, Yelp decided to publicly shame those stores, salons, restaurants, and bars that had attempted to pay for reviews by posting a notice to the offending businesses' pages:

> **Consumer Alert:** We caught someone red-handed trying to buy reviews for this business. We weren't fooled, but wanted you to know because buying reviews not only hurts consumers, but also honest businesses who play by the rules. Check out the evidence here . . .

Yelp then published the e-mail strings between business owners and the undercover Yelper to prove its case.

TripAdvisor, like other review sites, uses a computer algorithm to predict when posted content on its site is likely to be fake. These code-based tools look at everything from the IP address (unique Internet protocol address) used by reviewers to a linguistic analysis of review text to determine when a review might not be legitimate. As it turns out, it is possible to tell the difference between most real and fake reviews.

Spot the Fake

Below are examples of a truthful review and a fake review generated through Amazon's Mechanical Turk program of a Hilton Hotel in Chicago. Can you guess which is which?

Review #1:

> This hotel is located right in the hustle and bustle of the city of Chicago. It is ideal for the corporate executive. Not only in terms of location but the hotel offers a spectacular view of the ocean. The dining room is spacious and makes eating at this hotel a really pleasant experience. While dining the guest experiences a nice ambiance as they overlook the city, which is picturesque especially at night, when the city lights come on. The rooms are nice and spacious and allows the guest to get all their work done with a desk area. I would strongly recommend this hotel for the corporate executive!

Review #2:

> went to chicago for a week in may, decided to be good to ourselves and stay in the hilton, we were not disapointed. perhaps it was becuse there were quite a few conventions going on and a lot of people were only staying 1 or 2 nights but we got upgraged to exceutive level. we had 2 double beds with a bathroom each. the beds and pillows were too die for, so so comfy ant the end of a day when we seemed to have walked for miles. all the staff were

very helpful. a lot of guests seemed to ignore the staff especially the chamber maids who they seemed to think they were in their way so perhaps that why some people felt these people were rude or unhelpful. about 2 blocks away on Harrison is a cafe called "Orange" which you have to make the only place you will have breakfast, the cafe and the staff are suberb. expect a 15 min wait on a sat & sun morning.[22]

Research scientist Myle Ott and his colleagues set out to solve this problem by developing an algorithm to detect what he called "deceptive opinion spam."[23] To aid in their research, Ott and his team created a publicly accessible data set of 800 reviews of twenty hotels in the Chicago area, with 400 reviews being validated, truthful reviews culled from TripAdvisor's set of 6,977 reviews of the subject "20 Chicago Hotels,"[24] eliminating non-five-star reviews, non-English reviews, short reviews (less than 150 characters), and reviews written by first-time reviewers. To amass fake reviews, Ott's team used Amazon's Mechanical Turk program, the same task-based marketplace allegedly used as a tool for fake-review-writing firms.

Ott paid writers one dollar for a fake review and limited each reviewer to writing just one. In the instructions, Ott provided the name of the hotel and a link to the property's Web site. He asked each reviewer to assume the role of an employee in the hotel's marketing department who was asked by management to post a fake review. They were also asked to write a review that sounded realistic and portrayed the hotel in a positive light. Ott's team, by using computational linguistics, was able to distinguish between authentic and fake reviews 90 percent of the time.[25]

From my experience, many proponents of online reviews believe that the presence of fake reviews is negated by the fact that most consumers can see past a phony online critique. Data gathered during Ott's study disputes that finding. To measure the effectiveness of human judgment on the validity of the TripAdvisor reviews, Ott had three graduate students assess the reviews, and asked them to identify valid versus fake reviews. The three students didn't do as well as the algorithm, getting between 53 and 61.9 percent right,[26] far below the performance of the linguistic-based computer analysis.

In looking at the differences between accurate versus deceptive reviews, a few come to light that might help in detection. In the past the common perception was that deceptive reviews tend to have a decreased usage of first-person singular (e.g., I, me, mine). Previous research indicates that this is due to individuals wanting to distance themselves from their fraudulent reviews. In Ott's study, increased usage of the first-person pronoun increased the likelihood of a deceptive review. Why the switch? Ott speculates that with deceptive reviews, the reviewer is trying to bolster credibility by emphasizing their relation to the review.

The study also found that truthful reviews tend to include "more sensorial and concrete language than deceptive opinions." For example, the valid reviews had more specifics about spatial configurations than the fake reviews. So if a review tended to explain room configuration or sizes or locations of things, that review was more likely to be valid.

Did you guess which review was authentic and which was false? The Mechanical Turk contractor generated the first review, while the second was a valid TripAdvisor review. Fake reviews are usually descriptive and tend to use superlatives and personal pronouns. The misspellings and improper capitalization should have tipped you off to the real versus fraudulent review.

The Problem of Situational Bias

While a negative review might result in a lost $20 gadget sale on Amazon or a $9.99 movie download, in the case of reviews on TheFunded, the stakes can be in the millions. The site provides reviews on more than six thousand venture capital funds and thirteen thousand partners. Entrepreneur Adeo Ressi started the site in 2006 after a relationship with a $3 million investor in a $9 million round went sour. Ressi realized that entrepreneurs were choosing venture funds and partners based on reputation and hearsay.[27] TheFunded provides entrepreneurs with a forum to share both their experience in getting funded by venture capital as well as their experience working with the firm's partners after investment.

Sharam Fouldager-Mercer, an entrepreneur who just closed a $4 million Series A round for his start-up AirPR, is a frequent visitor to TheFunded. According to Fouldager-Mercer, the site is a great resource for entrepreneurs who are new to funding and venture capital. In the past, the inner workings of a VC felt as though it were shrouded in secrecy. Today, sites like TheFunded, which are influenced by situational bias, provide a glance into this high-stakes world. Sharam does point out an issue with the reviews on the site. TheFunded is a great resource, but its very strength creates its very weakness. Due to the anonymity of the site, the user doesn't know the perspective of the reviewer. Are they merely angry because they weren't funded? Are they happy merely because they were? As a result, it can be hard to determine the value of the review. With the entrepreneurs of successful start-ups making their funding decisions based on reviews on the site, a series of bad reviews that might be biased by those reviewers who did not receive funds from the reviewed could result in the loss of a multimillion-dollar deal.

Another form of situational bias presents itself for businesses that provide a utilitarian service. How often do you wake up, turn on the light in your kitchen, and think to yourself, "I need to go online and give PG&E (or Con Edison) a five-star review. Every time I flip a light switch my lights come on"? I'm guessing the answer is never. Your utility provider probably has mostly negative reviews. The only time you will visit an online review site for your power company is when there is a prolonged power outage or if you had a long wait time on hold or an unsatisfactory appointment.

RateMyProfessors is another example of a ratings site that is prone to situational bias. The site, which was founded in 1998, has grown to now house a database of 14 million ratings on 1.3 million professors at more than seven thousand schools. The site allows students to rate their college instructors on overall quality, clarity, helpfulness, easiness, and, of course, hotness. The site suffers from the same situational bias as TheFunded. If a student provides a low rating to a professor due to a poor grade, the professor might be at fault, but other likely conclusions are that the student didn't apply himself, didn't study, or possibly didn't have the aptitude for the class.

When Reviews Have Nothing to Do with Their Subject

Political Motivation

Before the presidential elections in September 2012, Barack Obama made an unannounced visit to Big Apple Pizza in Fort Pierce, Florida. Scott Van Duzer, the owner of the restaurant, gave the president a big bear hug, lifting him off the ground. The press photographers following the president on the campaign trail snapped the photo, which went viral. Views of the image, and national media coverage of the hug, weren't the only things to go viral; so did Big Apple Pizza's Yelp reviews. Prior to the president's visit, the pizza parlor had a paltry two reviews; within a few days of the visit that number had skyrocketed to more than twenty-five hundred.[28] The problem of course was that most of those reviews had nothing to do with the quality of Big Apple's pizza and everything to do with politics. One-star reviews flooded in from the right, opposing the presidential hug from an owner who happened to be a registered Republican, then five-star ratings came in from the left. Hug-Gate created the perfect example of reviews that have nothing to do with the subject of the review, and everything to do with controversy.

In a demonstration of how fast social media can move to correct an injustice, soon after the flood of politically motivated reviews posted to Big Apple's Yelp page, a petition was circulated asking Yelp to remove the postings. Those reviews have now all been removed.

Comic Relief

If you're in the market for a banana slicer, you should check out the Hutzler 571 Banana Slicer. As of this writing, the slicer has amassed 4,593 reviews. Few, if any, of those reviewers have actually bought or tried this product. The Hutzler is one of many products on Amazon that are targets for faux reviews. In the previous chapter we discussed self-expression as a motivation for writing online reviews. This motivation is the primary driver for so many who want to demonstrate their comedic writing skills. For example, take this review by SW3K:

> For decades I have been trying to come up with an ideal way to slice a banana. "Use a knife!" they say. Well . . . my parole officer won't allow me to be around knives. "Shoot it with a gun!" Background check . . . HELLO! I had to resort to carefully attempt to slice those bananas with my bare hands. 99.9% of the time, I would get so frustrated that I just ended up squishing the fruit in my hands and throwing it against the wall in anger. Then, after a fit of banana-induced rage, my parole officer introduced me to this kitchen marvel and my life was changed.

No longer consumed by seething anger and animosity towards thick-skinned yellow fruit, I was able to concentrate on my love of theatre and am writing a musical play about two lovers from rival gangs that just try to make it in the world. I think I'll call it South Side Story.

Or this review from Mrs. T.:

What can I say about the 571B Banana Slicer that hasn't already been said about the wheel, penicillin, or the iPhone. . . . this is one of the greatest inventions of all time. My husband and I would argue constantly over who had to cut the day's banana slices. It's one of those chores NO ONE wants to do! You know, the old "I spent the entire day rearing OUR children, maybe YOU can pitch in a little and cut these bananas?" and of course, "You think I have the energy to slave over your damn bananas? I worked a 12 hour shift just to come home to THIS?!" These are the things that can destroy an entire relationship. It got to the point where our children could sense the tension. The minute I heard our 6-year-old girl in her bedroom, re-enacting our daily banana fight with her Barbie dolls, I knew we had to make a change. That's when I found the 571B Banana Slicer. Our marriage has never been healthier, AND we've even incorporated it into our lovemaking. THANKS 571B BANANA SLICER!

From fraudulent and sham reviews to conflicts of interest, extortion, differing viewpoints, or faux reviews, there are numerous reasons why you might decide to turn a blind eye toward online reviews. Doing so, however, would be a mistake. You might be asking yourself, with all of the problems with reviews, why should I pay any attention to these sites?

We know that almost 80 percent of consumers say they consult online reviews before making a purchase decision.[29] We also know that the volume of online reviews is growing at a very strong pace. Yes, there are very good reasons to hate reviews. Ignoring them, however, will cost you customers and significant revenue. In order to survive, online review sites will have to improve their ability to find and eliminate fake and sham reviews. Algorithms will improve over time to spot fake postings.

Although valid negative reviews are a small minority of all reviews, business owners still have a hard time dealing with criticism. Bad reviews happen. In the next chapter I'll discuss how to get over your avoidance of negative reviews and turn criticism into a learning opportunity.

3

★ ★ ★ ★ ★

Bad Reviews Happen

★ ★ ★ ★ ★

You may have picked this book up because you're a small-business owner and have had a bad experience with reviews, or maybe you're a curious customer, or perhaps a marketer at a large corporation interested in understanding how to leverage online reviews for your company. No matter what your motivation, here's a useful exercise for understanding how reviews work and how you can leverage them.

Do this now: Put this book down and get on the Internet. Open your browser and visit Yelp. While you might want to immediately check in on your own business's ratings, we're going to start by studying another business first. Consider this an exercise in desensitization, much like fear-of-flying courses desensitize fearful flyers by putting them in planes that initially taxi around the airport without ever leaving the ground.

In the "Find" box at the top of Yelp's page, type in "restaurant," and in the location box titled "Near," type in your zip code or the closest city, then click on the search icon to the right.

On the results page from the search you just executed, you should see a list of the restaurants closest to you and the average Yelp ranking, in stars, for each restaurant. If you happen to live in a small town and don't see any restaurants with reviews, choose the nearest larger city and perform the same search.

Find a restaurant that you have been to before, but don't click through just yet.

Take out a blank piece of paper. Create two columns by drawing a line down the length of the paper and label the columns "pros" and "cons." Before reading any reviews, from your own experience list things that stand out as positives for this particular establishment in the pros column; be as specific as possible (e.g., your favorite dish at the restaurant, something positive about the ambience, the service). Now do the same thing for the cons column (e.g., dishes that you didn't like, problems with service, other things that turned you off about the restaurant).

When you've finished, click on the restaurant's name in Yelp to access their reviews. Sort the reviews by ranking, going through the first five highest reviews for the establishment. Using the same sheet of paper, or a new two-column page if you were prolific with your own assessment of the restaurant, list some of the recurring positive comments that appear in their top five reviews. Now do the same for the worst reviews of that restaurant (you can get there by going to the bottom of the page and clicking on the last page number). Now look for specific negative comments from the bottom five reviews and list in your cons column the recurring issues that reviewers had.

Once you've finished, look back to your original list. First, how similar were the pros and cons of the restaurant between your observations and the aggregate observations of Yelp reviewers? Did you find any similarities? Having dined at this particular restaurant, did you find that there was undeserved praise—or unwarranted criticism? Were there comments that you didn't jot down in your assessment that you found to be true? A dish or service person you didn't remember offhand, or perhaps an observation that just never occurred to you? How wide is the variance in reviews? Did some diners give it a five-star review while others opted for a one- or two-star review?

When you surveyed reviews for a specific business you probably noticed that customers of the same business might have had wildly different experiences, from one-star disasters to five-star "most memorable experience ever." Did the diners eat at the same restaurant? One of the biggest complaints about Yelp and other review sites is that the reviews are not fair or accurate. If you've been avoiding reading your own reviews because of the lack of accuracy and fairness, I'm going to help you get over that.

If you found that there were some items that were eye-openers for you on the aggregate Yelp reviews (some things that you had forgotten about or just hadn't considered), then you have just experienced one of the hidden values of online reviews, that often the aggregate opinion of online reviewers can reveal perspectives that you might have missed. In the pages that follow you will see that by broadening your focus away from just the negative reviews, you will start to see patterns emerge from the collective reviews of a business that will provide you with insights for your business, your competition, your industry, or even your favorite restaurant.

Coming to Terms with Bad Reviews

I can understand the desire to shield yourself from negative reviews. I did exactly that when I took a five-year break from writing.

I can still remember my first negative review. I was sitting at my kitchen island, the same place that I spent hours researching and writing my first book, *Click*. Waking at five in the morning and working after midnight night after night finishing a manuscript, there's a lot of anticipation building up toward the book's release date. It might not surprise you to hear that most authors, including this one, obsess over Amazon rankings and consumer reviews on Amazon, Barnes & Noble, Goodreads, and other sites.

"Obvious Information, Boring, and an Ad for the Author" read the title of one review that was penned the week after my book launched. My critic "Eco-Friendly Interior Designer" wrote: "I was too bored and disgusted with the author's writing about himself to do anything but half-heartedly skim through." My mood changed, from eager anticipation for that day's television and radio interviews that had been lined up to promote the book to instant and crushing feelings of self-doubt. It didn't matter that of my seventy-six reviews, forty-eight had four or five stars. It didn't matter that my book hit the *New York Times* best-seller list that week.

While up until that morning I had enjoyed reading my reviews on the various book review sites, at that moment I stopped reading what critics had to say about *Click*. As I began writing this manuscript, I conducted the same exercise that I asked you to complete at the beginning of this chapter. At first the exercise was difficult; rereading the negative reviews, I was transported back to my kitchen island in October 2005. As I analyzed both positive and negative reviews I began to see patterns in the criticism: "the book is too promotional," "the author talks too much about himself," "the book is an exercise in navel-gazing."[1] I put that negative criticism in perspective and began to realize that there was some truth to the critiques. More important, I was able to launch a new writing project with some direction into how I could improve.

When I started to interview business owners for this book, I was struck by how all conversations gravitated toward a discussion of a specific negative review and the conclusion that online reviews are worthless. It was during those interviews that I realized that the business owners I had been talking with were feeling the same way I had after reading my one- and two-star book reviews.

Criticism, especially if it's unfounded, inaccurate, or vindictive, is very difficult to digest. But reading negative reviews can have a positive effect on your business. Every valid negative point in a review has the potential for helping you improve your business. Think of it not as criticism but as data.

Over the last ten years I've built a career around online competitive intelligence, helping clients leverage online behavioral data to improve their own businesses. The amount of consumer behavioral and competitive intelligence that is available just by reading reviews of your business and your competitors' is staggering. It's not unlike having access to customer satisfaction survey responses for your closest competitors. Why wouldn't you want to distill what works and doesn't work for other businesses in your industry? If you've decided to turn a blind eye to reviews because of some unfair, biased, or outright fraudulent reviews, then you need to come to terms with one of the first imperatives of online review analysis: bad reviews happen, and you need to deal with them, learn from them, and, if possible, leverage them, or else move on.

Here's another exercise I'd like you to complete, this time to help you get over your negative reviews. Take any business considered to be the best in its field—the most critically acclaimed, the most profitable, the most successful. Now open your Internet browser, navigate to the most appropriate review site, and find their one-star reviews. I'm confident in saying that if the business or product is popular enough, there will be negative reviews. Now read those reviews.

One of my favorite books on economics, in fact my inspiration to write my first book, *Click*, was *Freakonomics* by Steven Levitt and Stephen Dubner. *Freakonomics* sold more than 4 million copies in thirty-five languages, and spent more than one hundred weeks on the *New York Times* best-seller list, capturing the coveted number-one position for many of those weeks. Yet if you read the book's 2,126 reviews on Amazon (as of this writing), this best seller received a staggering 143 one-star reviews.

Reviewer Drew titles his critique on Amazon "Over-rated and Simplistic," while another reviewer entitles his review "A Dangerous Abuse of Statistics." In total, 254 reviews for this breakout best seller were one- or two-star reviews.

Another example would be the best restaurant that you can think of. In my case it would have to be the restaurant that I took my wife to for our ten-year anniversary, a small intimate restaurant in the epicurean epicenter of northern California wine country. Thomas Keller's The French Laundry in Yountville, California, is one of the highest critically rated restaurants in the world. The restaurant has won the James Beard Award for Outstanding Service, has been named one of *Restaurant Magazine's* top fifty restaurants of the world, has been awarded three stars from the *Michelin Guide* every year since 2006, and was declared the best restaurant in the world by the ever-critical Anthony Bourdain.[2] The restaurant is so popular that reservations are made sixty days in advance. With such an amazing reputation, proven by the absolute calling frenzy each morning to score a reservation, you would think that all of The French Laundry's reviews would have to be five stars. You would be wrong.

Ask J.L. from Santa Clarita about his experience; he gives the restaurant one star. In his one-star review on Yelp, J.L. writes:

> This is my first review and felt compelled too because of my experience calling to make a reservation. How hard is it to call this place?! I have tried calling from 10am– 1042am pacific time and all i get is a busy tone. And when i finally get through, they tell me they are fully booked and i need to be put on a wait list . . . UNBELIEVABLE. This after trying for 2 straight days! I will have to wait and see if I ever get a call back from the wait list. Good luck to those securing a reservation.

J.L. gives The French Laundry one star simply because the restaurant is so popular that he can't get a reservation. From reading his short missive, you could assume that J.L. has never eaten at The French Laundry, yet his one-star review factors into the restaurant's overall review rating.

One of restaurant owners' top complaints is negative reviews when the reviewer hasn't even tried their establishment.

- I couldn't get a reservation—one star

- I couldn't get a parking spot—one star

- I can't afford this restaurant—one star

There are still some one-star reviews on Yelp and TripAdvisor among those lucky few who are able to score a reservation at the Yountville restaurant. Take the opinion of R.U.; out of 588, he holds one of the 51 one-star reviews on the top travel review site:

> To whoever reads this—go to the french laundry at your own risk, but don't say you weren't warned. It will be the biggest waste of $300 PER PERSON you will ever spend.

> ANYBODY who can grill a steak or chop carrots could cook this food. The owner of this restaurant should be ashamed of himself charging what he does in this economy for this crap.[3]

Three blocks down Washington Street from The French Laundry is Ciccio, a casual pizzeria that no doubt serves wonderful food. Dishes at Ciccio range from $8 for an appetizer to

$12 to $15 for an entrée or a pizza, while dinner at The French Laundry can be more than $295 before wine and tip. With an overall ranking of five stars, Ciccio bests Thomas Keller's flagship restaurant. Based on Yelp rankings in Yountville, should you expect a better dining experience at Ciccio or at The French Laundry?

I would like to tell you that I have the secret formula to ensure that you never get a negative review, but I don't. Whether you're Thomas Keller reading the reviews of your restaurant on Yelp or OpenTable or you're Joe of Joe's Bar and Grill, you will most likely have negative reviews, maybe even a few one-star reviews. The sooner that you can accept that fact, the sooner you will be able to take the next step in leveraging crowdsourced opinions to better your business.

Extraordinary Lengths

Some businesses will go to extraordinary lengths to suppress online reviews. Take the case of New York dentist Dr. Stacy M. and her patient Robert L.

Robert sought out the services of Dr. M. due to an extremely sore tooth. Before seeing Robert, Dr. M. insisted that he sign several forms, including a form entitled "Mutual Agreement to Maintain Privacy." The form, which he signed, stated that he would not write anything disparaging about the dentist.[4]

After a billing dispute arose between Robert and Dr. M.'s practice, he wrote a negative review on Yelp:

> Avoid at all cost! Scamming their customers! Overcharged me by about $4000 for what should have been only a couple hundred dollar procedure. Refuses to submit the claim to my insurance company. When asked for records to submit the claim myself they referred me to a 3rd party that wants 5% of the bill ($268) to get the records for me. By law the dentist must give me the records within 10 days of written request at a cost of no more than 75 cents per page. Lawsuit to be filed soon

Robert then received a letter from the doctor's office demanding that he delete the post and threatening a lawsuit for breach of contract. He also received an invoice for one hundred dollars per day that the Yelp review remained on the site.[5] More than two years later, the review remains on Yelp.

While the dentist's breach-of-contract approach was novel, as few businesses to date have attempted to contractually limit their clients' ability to publicly criticize them, other attempts by businesses to suppress online reviews have been overwhelmingly ineffective given the power of the First Amendment and freedom of speech.

There are a lot of reasons why bad reviews happen, but sometimes those bad reviews are actually earned. Next time you're in Boston, be careful when choosing your pizza delivery service.

When Bad Reviews Are Accurate

Bad reviews can be a sign of bad business. With twenty-one one-star ratings out of twenty-one total reviews, the Regal Café Pizzeria in Boston, Massachusetts, could possibly be one of the worst businesses ranked on Yelp and is a good example of when online reviews reveal the true character of an operation.

Reading through all the reviews of the Boston pizzeria reveals a repeating scenario. Business travelers, checking into their hotel late at night, hungry after a long day of travel, ask their front-desk clerk where they can get some food. The clerk provides the traveler with a menu that offers food delivered twenty-four hours a day. The restaurant offers everything from pizza to sandwiches, chicken wings, fried mozzarella sticks, seafood dinners, and tiramisu and cheesecake for dessert.

The hungry traveler orders a pizza for thirteen dollars and waits for his order to arrive. According to most reviewers, after a significant delay, the delivery person arrives with a pizza, wings, cheesecake, a salad. The traveler informs the delivery person that he didn't order all of this extra food. He's assured that the food is a gift from the restaurant, which is either celebrating something or has extra food, and it's being provided at no extra charge. When the traveler checks his credit card statement days or weeks later he discovers that his thirteen-dollar pizza cost anywhere from sixty-five to eighty dollars. The details of the delivery scam are so similar that it might seem like the Regal Café is the target of a review-bombing campaign by a ruthless competitor.

The local Boston CBS news affiliate learned of numerous complaints to the state's attorney general's office and launched an I-Team investigation. In order to verify complaints that they heard, the I-Team ordered pizza, and, like the reviewers had recounted, the driver showed up with extra food, stating that the extras were from a Halloween party and were complimentary. An eighteen-dollar bill later resulted in credit card charges from Regal Café for more than eighty-four dollars.[6]

From Regal's perfect one-star record on Yelp to the yearly winner of TripAdvisor's worst hotel (a practice that the site discontinued in 2012 to "stay more positive"), it's clear that some negative reviews are well earned. At a minimum, negative reviews can reveal areas for improvement and help bolster consumer trust in your positive reviews.

While writing this chapter, I revisited my negative reviews on Amazon and Goodreads. More than five years since my first book was released, it's still difficult to read through some of the critical and, in some cases, dismissive comments from readers. That being said, Eco-Friendly Interior Designer had made some valid points about my writing. I did rely too heavily on one source of data. Did that create an end product that might be interpreted as a commercial? Absolutely. Was my first book an exercise in navel gazing, as one reviewer commented? Sure, I can see how someone might come away with that conclusion. I now keep a list of common criticisms, challenge myself to address them, and return to those reviews to come up with ways of improving. It's hard not to think of how you will review this book, but this time I plan to be more receptive to reviews, both positive and negative.

4

★ ★ ★ ★ ★

Who Writes Reviews

★ ★ ★ ★ ★

Back at Gloria's All-Star Barbershop, Gloria announces that I'm writing a book about online reviews and proceeds to ask her waiting customers what they think about Yelp. Since her shop is on the main drag in downtown San Mateo, her clientele are usually a mix of local businessmen, owners of restaurants, real estate agents, insurance salesmen, and shop owners.

A local real estate agent, leafing through an old *Sports Illustrated*, looks up and says, scowling, "Just a bunch of complainers." The other patron, who's busy texting, chimes in without looking up, "They're just a bunch of angry people. They use Yelp as a place to bully us business owners." Gloria launches into her rant about one of her reviews that she knows is fake, and I start to zone out, as I've heard this story at least twenty times. I begin to wonder what motivates individuals to interrupt their normal daily activity to go online and pen reviews.

Reviews can span from a few sentences written on a smartphone to longer, well-thought-out productions that include pictures and, in the case of some reviewers, well-produced video commentary. Are reviewers driven by anger, self-promotion, the hopes of receiving free goods and services, or are they more altruistic, hoping to warn the community about a bad experience and reward a business for an excellent product or service?

Let's start with data to understand the demographic and psychographic of who writes reviews. I work as the general manager of global research for Experian Marketing Services, where I spend most of my workday combing through mountains of consumer behavioral data to understand what drives people to do what they do. Two key data sets that I work with on a daily basis are the Experian Marketing Services data set, which provides aggregate information on what 5 million U.S. Internet users are doing each day, what sites are they visiting, and what search terms they use; and the Experian National Consumer Study, a survey-based research tool featuring responses from more than twenty-five thousand consumers in the United States and data on more than sixty thousand different elements.

My first question: how many consumers review products and services online? According to our 2013 data, 11.2 percent of our sample reported that they post ratings and reviews online for others to read. Extrapolated to the general population, that would equate to more than 25.3 million consumers posting reviews. When I wrote *Click* in 2008, a separate study indicated that only 1 percent of the population was writing online reviews. Based on those two data sets, there has been a tenfold increase in review writers in less than five years. While I'm sure the gentleman in Gloria's shop is correct when he says some complainers use online review sites as a means to channel their aggression, I doubt that they make up the majority of the 25 million posters, especially considering that only 13 percent of the reviews on Yelp are one-star reviews.[1]

The second question: who are these reviewers? Are there specific demographics by age, gender, and household income that make up the bulk of online reviewers? Many business owners assume that only young, technically proficient consumers are the ones writing reviews. While the data does show a skew toward younger consumers, there's a lot of nuance to the reviewers' demographic makeup.

For example, reviewers skew ever so slightly female, with women coming in at 51.7 percent and men at 48.3 percent. And reviewers are slightly younger than the population as a whole, with the largest age bin group of reviewers falling between 25 and 34 years of age and accounting for 30.2 percent of all reviews. If you're in this age group you're 73 percent more likely to have reviewed products and services online than the population as a whole.

Of all ethnicities, Caucasians index in line with the population for writing reviews, as do African Americans, while Hispanics index below the population as a whole for penning their criticisms on online review sites. One ethnicity outranks all others in review writing per capita—Asian Americans, who are more than 60 percent more likely to write an online review than the overall population.

Audience measurement firm Quantcast estimates that 15 percent of Yelpers are Asian American, an impressive number when you consider that Asian Americans make up only 5 percent of the U.S. population.[2] In an article in *Hyphen* magazine, columnist Victoria Yue explored reasons why Asian Americans might Yelp (the act of reviewing businesses on the site has become a verb) more than the population as a whole. She postulates that since the San Francisco Bay Area has a high concentration of Asian Americans, and Yelp is based in San Francisco, that could explain part of the overrepresentation of one group. While that might explain the plethora of Asian American reviewers in one geographical area, it could also be that many Asian Americans match the demographic of Yelp reviewers: highly educated, young professionals with greater access to technology than the population as a whole.[3]

Of all the demographics that I analyzed, however, there is one particular group that was the most prolific in writing reviews, and the most likely to read and consider reviews in making their purchase decisions.

Power Reviewers—the Mom Factor

The most prolific demographic of individuals who read and write online reviews isn't age range, geography, or gender, but, rather, life stage. Young parents, specifically moms with children from birth to five years of age, are eight times more likely than the population as a whole to write reviews.

This might seem like a random segment to index the highest of any demographic that measured in the data set (more than sixty thousand different data elements), but moms with young children are experiencing one of the most significant life changes, and one with a dizzying array of product and service choices. Think of all the questions and concerns that must bombard the new mother: What crib should I buy? What are the best wipes? Which pediatrician should I use? Which cereals are the best? Where is the best day care? In the age before online reviews, a new mom would rely on the recommendations of family and friends, but today, perhaps due to convenience, the quest to find more robust opinions, or maybe to avoid asking questions that might be perceived as embarrassing, new moms are reading online reviews and sharing their knowledge by writing reviews for the benefit of others.

The data also indicates that this specific segment is the most socially connected online, regularly visiting Facebook, Pinterest, and mom-specific social networks like CafeMom. Moms with young children are also heavy mobile Internet users, spending a good portion of their online day accessing their Facebook pages, e-mail, and texting while out. The combination of mobile and social online activity is powerful in the world of online reviews as this particular group is likely to read and write them at the point of purchase, whether it's showrooming (the act of checking prices and reviews online while in a physical store), other forms of research, or writing a review on the spot.

Even if you don't cater to this demographic, look to moms with young children as the early adopters of online review sites and behaviors. What they're doing online today will likely spread to the rest of the population in a very short period of time.

Online Review Users Are More Affluent

Visitors to online review sites (including Yelp, TripAdvisor, Angie's List, and others) are more affluent than the population as a whole. In fact there is a strong positive correlation between income level and likelihood to visit online review sites. Internet users who have household incomes less than $30,000 per year are 21 percent less likely than the population to visit online reviews sites, while those users who earn more than $150,000 per year are 95 percent more likely than the population to frequent online review sites.

The affluence skew could be explained by the fact that consumers with more money are more likely to travel, and more likely to buy products and services that are apt to be reviewed, like restaurant meals and electronics. As I go through the Mosaic segmentation for all the major online reviews sites, what becomes very noticeable is that the top segment for each site is affluent customers.

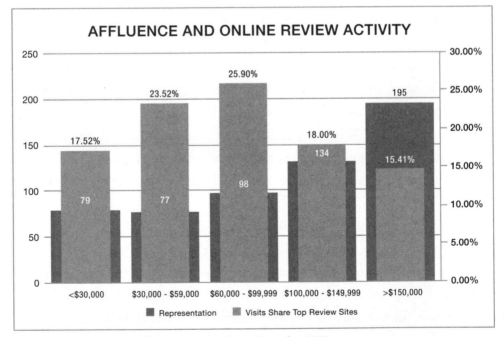

AFFLUENCE AND ONLINE REVIEW ACTIVITY

Legend: Representation ■ Visits Share Top Review Sites

Data points: <$30,000: 79, 17.52% | $30,000 - $59,000: 77, 23.52% | $60,000 - $99,999: 98, 25.90% | $100,000 - $149,999: 134, 18.00% | >$150,000: 195, 15.41%

Source: Experian Marketing Services Data, December 2013

If your business caters to affluent customers, you should incorporate online reviews into your own Web site; failing to do so could result in consumers leaving your site to visit other online review sites before they make their purchase decisions. One of the most important rules in e-commerce: don't give consumers a reason to leave your site before they've completed the transaction.

Reviewer Difference by Review Site

Not all reviewers are created equal. In fact, depending on which online review site you're analyzing, there can be dramatic differences in income levels, geodemographics, and, as we will see below, age. Angie's List, which was founded in 1995, has differentiated itself from Yelp by offering a service without an advertiser conflict of interest (Angie's List is primarily a subscription-based service where the consumer pays for access to reviews). Angie's List's focus is around service providers, mostly home repair and home contractors, but also doctors, dentists, and accountants.

The average age of Angie's List customers is much older than Yelp's customer base. By checking the Mosaic geodemographics, we find that the top two groups visiting Yelp are Young City Solos, a group of young active singles living in metropolitan areas, and the Power Elite, the most affluent couples in the country, living in the most exclusive areas. Together these two groups account for 12 percent of Yelp's traffic. The top two groups for Angie's List, making up 23 percent of all site visitors, also include the Power Elite, as well as a group called Booming with Confidence, wealthy baby boomers living in suburban areas. Overall, visitors to Angie's List tend to be older than Yelpers. TripAdvisor has far more visitors between the ages of 35 and 44, and 65 plus, while Yelp dominates the 25-to-34-year-old category.

Geographics: What Cities Index the Highest?

Seven of the top ten cities indexing the highest for visits to online review sites are in California; in fact; with the exception of Honolulu and Austin, Texas, they are all on the West Coast.

Top Ten DMAs® for Online Review Visits/population (December 2013):

1. San Francisco, California

2. San Diego, California

3. Honolulu, Hawaii

4. Los Angeles, California

5. Monterey-Salinas, California

6. Santa Barbara, California

7. Austin, Texas

8. Palm Springs, California

9. Sacramento, California

10. Seattle-Tacoma, Washington

Source: Experian Marketing Services

While it might seem that critical mass in online review postings has been reached, worldwide data indicates that U.S. review posters are less than a third per capita compared to India and China.

According to Forrester Research, the United States is far behind the leaders of online review postings. In metropolitan India and Mainland China, more than 70 percent of the population say that they post online reviews, while in the United States, online posters are just shy of 20 percent, or less than a third of India's and China's posters.[4] Given that moms with young children are eight times more likely to post reviews than the population as a whole, it's likely that this particular segment makes up a good portion of that 20 percent.

What Drives Reviews?

Knowing who your reviewers are is the first part of the puzzle. What motivates them to log on to an online review site and broadcast their opinions of your business is a much more complex matter. Several academics have written about the motivation behind reviews. Edward McQuarrie, a professor of marketing at Santa Clara University, writes about three primary motivations behind online reviews: solidarity, status, and the soapbox effect.[5]

McQuarrie notes that based on his research, reviewers are not motivated by the most common incentive, compensation. A common misconception among business owners is that reviewers have some ulterior motive in posting their online opinions.

Of course, there are some reviewers (McQuarrie would likely argue that this is a small minority) who do attempt to extort businesses for their own financial gain, but it seems that for the majority of reviewers, motivation comes from a slightly less selfish place.

Solidarity

The first motivation to review is for the sense of community or solidarity that review writing provides. In essence, McQuarrie argues that review sites like Yelp provide their reviewers with feedback mechanisms that foster reciprocity and build a sense of community. Reviewers can give back to their community by posting reviews about local businesses; they can also provide feedback on others' reviews. After reading a review a reader can comment, and vote on that review being funny, useful, or cool. Amazon and Google+ provide similar feedback tools. As McQuarrie identifies in his paper, Yelp provides a more significant feedback tool in that reviewers can provide feedback on other reviewers versus just on their reviews.

The community motivation to participate in online reviews is very similar to the motivation to participate on social networks like Facebook, where users post comments and then receive feedback in the form of likes and comments. The only difference, some might argue, is the addition of meaningful content generated by the user.

Status

The second motivation, according to McQuarrie's research, is status. Almost all major review sites have some form of status for high-volume reviewers. Yelp has its Elite badge, Amazon its top reviewers, and TripAdvisor its Top Contributors.

While some reviewers might be motivated solely by the pursuit of an elite-reviewer status level, most high-volume reviewers are also rewarded with more tangible benefits. Yelp Elite reviewers, for example, are invited to special Elite-only events in their area to sample the food, products, or services of local businesses. High-volume Amazon reviewers are often asked to join Amazon's Vine program, which provides free products to reviewers with the expectation that they will post reviews. Even TripAdvisor provides small gifts, such as luggage tags and tote bags, to its frequently posting reviewers.

Self-Expression

The third motivation is what McQuarrie calls autotelic behavior, or what he describes as an expressive rather than a utilitarian benefit. He cites play and art as examples of autotelic behaviors,[6] where the motivation to produce something is the reward of producing the content. Reviewers who are autotelic in nature might be described as individuals who take pride in the quality of their written reviews and the pictures they append to illustrate their points. A parallel to the autotelic reviewer would be the blogger, who might at some point receive some compensation for her work, but whose primary motivation is to produce engaging content for anyone who cares to read it.

While these three motivators go a long way to describe what drives most reviewers, I believe there is more complexity to what motivates people to spend their time writing reviews.

Elite Yelper Eric B.—Everyone Is Entitled to My Opinion

Sitting out in a courtyard of a small retail building in downtown Walnut Creek, California, I decide to cut to the chase with Eric B., a mild-mannered engineer who's been an Elite Yelper since 2008. His stats are impressive, with 4,213 reviews, 1,895 friends, and more than 29,700 votes for useful reviews. He's posted 2,100 pictures and racked up 1,178 firsts (being the first on Yelp to review a business).

When I ask Eric why he writes reviews he doesn't skip a beat. "Because I think everyone should be entitled to my opinion." He laughs, and I think he's joking. Talking with Eric B., it's clear that he takes great pride in his reviews, in their accuracy and their completeness.

Like many reviewers I've spoken with, Eric tells me that he views Yelp as his online diary. From that description, it sounds as though his reviews fit the autotelic category of motivations. He does confide that the sheer number of reviews he has penned might be the result of some compulsion to review every experience. A quick glance through his profile reveals reviews on everything from the usual restaurant and service businesses to parks, museums, even houses of worship. Looking at Eric's profile, I'm struck by how few one-star reviews he's authored since 2008; out of 4,213 reviews, only 8 were one-star reviews, or 0.2 percent.

Talking with Eric, it's clear that online reviews serve a utilitarian purpose, a way to record his own experiences as well as a place to discover new things to try. Beyond the utility, review sites such as Yelp also provide him with social interactions. While he doesn't attend quite as many Yelp Elite parties now as he has in the last five years as part of the Elite, he has formed offline friendships with other reviewers. According to Eric, who has penned 839 five-star reviews at the writing of this book, in order to earn that fifth star, a business has to do something that stands out; they have to go beyond the expected.

When comparing Eric to McQuarrie's three motivational drivers for reviews, status seeking doesn't appear to be a significant driver for Eric's prolific review writing but rather a by-product of his diligent work documenting his experiences. Eric's main drivers are the utility that online reviews provide as well as the sense of community he gets by contributing his opinions.

In a later study, McQuarrie analyzed the motivations of high-volume versus low-volume reviewers. He found that while low-volume reviewers were motivated by votes of usefulness, higher-volume reviewers like Eric were motivated by the idea of having a place to publish their writing and having an audience that would read their work.[7] McQuarrie also found that while low-volume reviewers were likely to write rants (one-star reviews) and raves (five-star reviews), higher-volume reviewers were less likely to produce extremely positive or negative reviews. While Eric also fills this profile, Ron C. in New York City has the tendency to go to an extreme.

Elite Yelper Ron C.—That's Just F'd Up

Ron was first introduced to Yelp when he moved from the San Francisco Bay Area to New York City. In 2008, the boss at Ron's first job in the city asked him to log on to Yelp, as he needed some reviews for his store to drive business. Ron decided not to write a review for his employer after consulting Yelp's guidelines, but serendipity led him through the site as he checked out the best places for Chinese food and other cuisines, and he began consulting Yelp as a city directory for his new hometown. In 2009, after being in the city for a year, he decided to start writing reviews.

Ron followed his passion for food and took a job at Mario Batali's food metropolis Eataly, a fifty-thousand-plus-square-foot food hall that bills itself as the largest artisanal Italian food and wine marketplace in the world. In his new position in the corporate offices for Eataly, Ron's job responsibilities include buying and receiving products for the store.

For Ron, the appeal in online reviews went beyond having an audience for his writing. Yelp became a professional resource to help him learn more about the New York City food scene. He saw the potential for market and competitive intelligence. Ron described how he would go on Yelp and look at pictures that were posted by other Yelpers to see what was going on without ever having to step foot in a competitor's market or restaurant.

For example, Ron wanted to see what other Italian restaurants that specialized in seafood were serving and then compare them to the offerings at Eataly. By reading descriptions and reviewing pictures from other Yelpers, he could get a good sense of the environment and food at a restaurant without sitting down and ordering a meal himself.

Ron also views his participation on Yelp as being career enhancing. For someone coming from outside the food industry, the Elite status that he's achieved on Yelp gave him street cred among the food professionals at Eataly.

I'm curious if Ron ever reads reviews for Eataly, as he is in a unique position of being an Elite Yelper while also being employed by a heavily reviewed retail food business. (Eataly, as of this writing, has 1,960 reviews and an average Yelp rating of three and a half stars.) It's apparent that he does. As Ron describes it, Eataly can be a victim of its own success when it comes to online reviews. The New York City mecca for Italian food is open long hours every day and is constantly busy. The restaurant and food hall can become so busy that some people leave and decide to give Eataly one or two stars just for being so popular.

Working in his position at the corporate office, Ron is also very familiar with the cost of the unique products that Eataly imports for its customers. He tells me some people complain that Eataly is too pricey, with cheeses that cost fourteen dollars a pound and some costing fifty-eight dollars a pound. Ron explains that some items in the store are expensive due to shipping and importing costs and that some reviewers don't understand that there's a reason why they are so expensive.

Ron says he writes reviews because he likes helping people,

providing opinions about places that people have questions about, and helping people figure out what to order and what not to order when they go to a restaurant. Ron describes himself as the kind of person who always gets asked directions on the street, and he likes to help people find where they want to go. Perhaps due to his experience seeing unjustified negative reviews for his employer, when Ron experiences lapses in service, his dark side emerges. Reading his one-star reviews, he's clearly not the person to cross.

In response to what it takes to get a five-star rating, Ron says, "Customer service is the most important thing to me. If I go in a restaurant and I'm not acknowledged or greeted, that's just f'd up." The restaurant that didn't greet him at the hostess station— one star. The second most important thing to Ron is how he's treated when he leaves.

Elite Reviewer Rebecca L.—Preserving the Memories

Rebecca is in her early thirties and works for the state of Washington in tax research and policy. When I ask Rebecca why she reviews on Yelp, her first response is that it's a great way to practice her writing skills. Before working in tax she was going to go to law school, and in her postcollege vortex she worried that if she didn't keep up with her writing she would lose her skill. As she looked for a good place to listen to jazz she discovered Yelp, and soon after started writing well-crafted reviews. Almost every place that she reviews she labels with a title. For her, titles are a way to emotionally connect to her subject matter and store her memories online. For example, she reviewed the restaurant Garden Korean Cuisine and titled it "Grandmother."

Here's an excerpt from Rebecca's review:

> My grandmother was an exceptional cook. It's because of her cooking that i got into food in the first place. She was the one that taught me how to make any food taste delicious and that care to your ingredients is where it starts. Even though my mother and i try to replicate her cooking, there's always something amiss . . . Our dishes are close to my dear departed granny, but it's not quite it. But Garden's spicy flounder stew is EXACTLY like my grandmother's cooking. and i mean, EXACTLY. In fact, it made me a bit teary because i didn't think i would taste anything like it again, but there it was, hidden away in a strip mall in Federal way, across the street from h-mart.
>
> That restaurant was a shock to me. I normally wouldn't have gone to this restaurant but my parents asked me to go to the restaurant. I tasted the dumplings and they tasted exactly like my grandmother's dumplings. Now whenever I want to remember my grandmother I will go back to this review.[8]

Like Eric B., Rebecca is writing reviews for her own purpose of keeping an online diary. She has a stronger emotional connection with Yelp as the place to store her memories. As we talk, I discover other important motivators for her reviews. Rebecca values the connections she's made with other reviewers. With the Yelp community being as big as it is, she feels that you're bound to find others who share the same tastes that you have. Rebecca knows which users' reviews are always spot-on, and that if they like a specific restaurant she'll like it as well. Another motivator that emerges is the friendships she's found from online reviews, and she proceeds to name other Elite Yelpers whom she considers her best friends.

Yelp makes Rebecca more connected to a community. There is something about sharing an experience, she says. Her time on Yelp has led her to try new things with her new foodie friends. Though she had never been to a Lebanese restaurant, fellow Yelpers Hannah L. and Shirley Y. convinced her to try a Seattle restaurant called Mamnoon, where she fell in love with a beet dip even though she thought she hated beets. This new experience helped Rebecca feel connected to Hannah and Shirley.

Using her influence to drive business for businesses that she's fond of is another key motivator for Rebecca. She wrote a review about a Korean restaurant in Linwood, and she was the first reviewer for this particular spot, a rare opportunity in the large Yelp community. According to Rebecca, what struck her about this place was how impeccable the service was. Because she was the first to review the restaurant, she started following their reviews, and brought all of her friends there. She wanted to see this restaurant succeed.

I asked Rebecca for her advice to businesses on getting the most out of review sites. Though she could not answer immediately, a few weeks later she answered that one of the best things a business could do is to use review sites to make experiences more memorable, that people write really positive or really negative reviews because something stood out and made them want to preserve that memory.

Top Amazon Reviewer Michael E.— Market Maker

Based in Syracuse, New York, Michael E. has reached rarefied air in the land of online reviews. Amazon hasn't released an official number of online reviewers, but some have noticed reviewers ranked as low as 17 million. Michael has risen above the masses and achieved the number-one position in Amazon's top reviewer ranking.

Michael got his big break in reviewing when he received an invitation to the Amazon Vine program. The program, which was launched in 2007, is an invitation-only group of customers selected by Amazon to review products, often before they are officially released. Vine members typically commit to reviewing two to four products per month that are sent to them free of charge. Michael's only commitment is that he must post a review within thirty days of receipt.

Initially he was picking a total of four products to review each month. With four reviews per month over the course of three years, his reviews started to add up. Before long he was getting multifunction laser printers, digital cameras, and other things that he really had an interest in. At one point, he received a spin bike valued at more than one thousand dollars. I was interested in how Michael was able to achieve such a high rank on Amazon.

In the beginning, when Michael first began reviewing on Amazon, he was ranked somewhere in the tens of thousands, but he eventually noticed that his rank was rising, and things started to get really interesting for him when he hit reviewer number 2,000. When he made the top 100 Amazon reviewers, Michael began posting video reviews, and his rank went up to the top 50. Once in the top 50, he added his e-mail address to his profile page and started to get e-mails daily, sometimes multiple times per day, asking him to review books or products.

I was curious about Michael's initial review. Before his competitive nature kicked in, what motivated him to write that first review? His first review was of a book on stock options on March 19, 2000. After reading the book, Michael realized that the reviews that convinced him to buy the book were more glowing than his assessment, and he wanted to set the record straight. Today, Michael's motivations haven't really changed.

"Even though with reviews I'm not selling anything, I am guiding people to make a good choice," he says.

Now that Michael is producing video reviews along with his text-based reviews, the process of reviewing a product can take as little as forty-five minutes to as long as the entire day, depending on how complex the product is. That doesn't count the amount of time that he uses the product to get a sense of how well it works; some products, like herbal supplements, can take weeks to review.

Once Michael is ready to review something that has been sent to him, he writes a script, videotapes his review, edits it, and then posts that review online. Michael is self-employed so he has more flexibility than someone who's working a nine-to-five job. There are some days when he works on reviews from the crack of dawn until late in the evening, reviewing as many as eight to ten products.

Talking to Michael, it's clear that his review activity is overtaking much of his daily life. He's searching for ways to make money from his activity. In fact, he gets paid to post reviews to Epinions, now owned by eBay. He's been exploring ways of monetizing his YouTube channel, yet I still don't get the impression that money is a primary motivation for Michael.

It's clear that as Michael has moved up in the rankings, the power that he has over the products he reviews is significant. After rating a product with just two stars, the company asked him to change his review as he was ruining their sales. Michael refused to change his rating and stands by his reviews. As Mc-Quarrie listed as the third motivation, Michael qualifies as an autotelic reviewer. Beyond reviewing for the pleasure of reviewing, I sense that Michael's competitive nature is a driving force as he shoots for the top. He was shocked to find himself in the top ten of all the millions of Amazon reviewers and explains that in the top ten everyone knows one another and everyone is keeping their eye on one another. By the end of 2013, Michael had landed the coveted number-one ranking among all Amazon reviewers.

When I ask Michael if he has any idea how the Amazon algorithm that ranks reviewers works, he responds that though there is a lot of speculation, nobody really knows. There are several components, such as the number of reviews authored by a reviewer, as well as the "helpful" and "unhelpful" hits that are made by for review readers to provide feedback on how useful a reviewer's comments are. Michael alludes to system gaming, where top reviewers try to knock down their "competition" by clicking on "not helpful" buttons of other reviewers.

Perhaps the motivations that drive reviewers are more complex than the three-part category that McQuarrie suggests. A sense of community is the most common reason that reviewers give for why they review.[9] The community tie is stronger for Yelp reviewers than it is for TripAdvisor and Amazon reviewers, which is likely due to the social-networking capabilities that exist within Yelp's site.

The common secondary motivation that surfaces among reviewers is the desire to help other people. What may not surface through qualitative research, due to cognitive dissonance, or the unwillingness of reviewers to admit it when asked, is that some are also driven by sheer competitiveness to be the top reviewer or to gain Elite status, as well as the reward of feeling important by being one of the top reviewers of an online review platform.

What I did take away from interviewing reviewers is that the Elite are predominantly benevolent in nature. Individuals who use reviews for retribution or seek to extort others or pad a business's reviews with unearned praise are the exception rather than the rule.

The Four Key Reviewer Archetypes and What They Mean to Your Business

Based on numerous academic studies and qualitative research, I've narrowed down online reviewer personalities into four main archetypes based on what motivates them to review.

Communitarian

The communitarian is the most predominant archetype for the elite-reviewer community. Despite the common misconception, Elite reviewers are not all status seekers; in fact, the majority of high-volume reviewers are more likely to be members of this group.

Key motivation: The communitarian is motivated by participating in the review community; his or her motivation would be equivalent to participating in a social network like Facebook, Google+, or Path. Communitarians build strong personal relationships with their friends and followers. Given the local nature of Yelp and Google+, a member of this group is more likely to participate in one of these networks rather than Amazon or TripAdvisor, which provide little incentive for offline friendships.

What you should know: Communitarians are one of the most important groups for a business to reach, as they tend to have elite status and the most friends or followers. While sites like Yelp provide a means to market toward these users via Elite events, your time and money would be better spent understanding who among your customers are Elite members and going out of your way to provide them with the highest possible quality of service. Given their influence in social media, time spent catering to this group will help spread their positive feedback.

Benevolent Reviewer

This particular archetype is the pleaser of the online review world; these reviewers understand the power of a positive review and like to help businesses that treat them well or with which they have a personal connection. The benevolent reviewer will often value personal connection over accuracy of review; in other words, they would be likely to write over-the-top praise for a restaurant if they liked the owner even if the establishment didn't warrant the praise.

Key motivation: This reviewer type likes to view their online review activity as a way of rewarding businesses that go out of their way to be friendly. In the pre-online-review world, the benevolent reviewer was an individual who would become a one-person volunteer marketing arm of their favorite in-town businesses.

What you should know: The benevolent reviewer is typically not a high-volume reviewer. Given the overall positive language and their limited history of other reviews, it's likely that services such as Yelp will filter their reviews. Just as with the other archetypes, it's not a good idea to directly ask a benevolent reviewer for a review, as they are likely to take offense. Just mentioning that your business is on TripAdvisor, Yelp, or Angie's List is enough to prime the pump.

Status Seeker

The status seeker is the competitive archetype. Increasing their status in the online world motivates them. The most common scenario for this group is the desire to attain Yelp Elite status. Even within the Yelp Elites, things can become competitive as the high-volume reviewers compete for bragging rights of who has written the most reviews, or has the greatest number of "useful" votes or other reviewers following them.

Key motivation: The driver for status seekers can vary among this group from the desire to attend Elite events to the thrill of competition. If a status seeker announces his status to you, it's likely that, at best, he's looking for special treatment or, at worst, he's malevolent and looking for free goods and services. Not all status seekers are bad; some just get caught up in the thrill of competition, like Michael E. The status seeker can also cross over into other archetypes.

What you should know: The status seeker as well as the communitarian are most likely to give unbiased reviews in their quest to increase their votes for useful review. (While not officially discussed, most reviewers believe that review site algorithms that determine elite top-reviewer status take usefulness votes into account.) Along those same lines, status seekers might embellish reviews with humor, pictures, or video to garner more "useful" votes.

One-Star Assassin

This group is the most dreaded of all reviewer types. They're easy to spot when you look at their distribution of reviews. Typically they will have predominantly one- and two-star reviews, and a few five-star reviews. Interestingly, this archetype doesn't see the point of a three-star review.

Key motivation: As the name implies, this group isn't looking for a community; they don't want to make anyone happy, and status means little. They view online review sites simply as a platform to air their grievances.

What you should know: In talking with business owners who have dealt with this group, there is often little warning as to which customers will turn into a one-star-slinging terror. It is likely that at some point you will encounter a one-star assassin. The best you can do is to listen to their complaints and, if they are valid, offer to make them right.

5

How Reviews, Even Bad Ones,
Are Good for You

★ ★ ★ ★ ★

This Place Sucks

Fueled by a few negative reviews he had received, James Beard
Award–winning chef and proprietor of Pizzeria Delfina, Craig
Stoll, decided to wage his own war against Yelp.

Visit Craig's restaurant on any night of the week and you're
likely to find that this "no reservation" San Francisco pizzeria
will have more than an hour wait for a table. Guests take their
places on the wait list by writing their names down in chalk on
a six-foot blackboard inside the restaurant's entryway. At peak
dinner hours you're likely to find a full blackboard and several
waiting diners huddled outside.

At the writing of this book, Pizzeria Delfina had 974 reviews
just for its California Street location in the Fillmore district (the
Mission location had 1,749). The majority of Yelp reviews on the
restaurant give the location four or five stars. A few, however, dif-
fer from the mainstream, grading the restaurant with one star.

Rather than reaching out to the disgruntled diners, or posting his own public response on Yelp, Stoll took the worst of his reviews and printed the negative comments in white on black shirts.

Waiters maneuver around packed tables with comments such as "the pizza was sooo greasy. I am assuming this was in part due to the pig fat" or "this place sucks" worn proudly across their chests.

Stoll doesn't read online reviews anymore. He gets so upset at the negative comments that he lets his business partner, and wife, monitor the restaurant's Yelp page. Stoll felt somewhat helpless in defending himself on forums like Yelp. There's no validation of reviews, and his critics can hide behind anonymity. His decision to make T-shirts for his staff was his way of venting his frustration as a business owner. Stoll went on to admit, during an NPR interview on the topic, that there were some useful suggestions that he gleaned by reading through his Yelp reviews. For example, some Yelpers were not happy with the small pasta portions served at the restaurant. Since Stoll intended the pasta portion as a first course, he made the portions appropriate to that purpose. The negative reviews allowed him to realize that this was a misunderstanding with his diners, and now they can order the pasta in either an appetizer or a main-course portion.

Competitive Intelligence

Competitive intelligence is a multibillion-dollar industry, with companies becoming very sophisticated in researching the internal and market practices of their competitive set. Operating a business without a clear picture of what's happening in the marketplace, specifically with direct competitors, is like flying with blinders on.

Running your business by looking only at your own data (cash receipts, Web analytics, comment cards, your own online reviews) and no external reference point is very similar to flying a plane into the clouds wearing foggles, or glasses with the upper half of the lenses fogged out. Of course with training or practice you could fly a plane with instruments alone, but why restrict yourself and risk making bad business decisions?

In today's world, where so much information is publicly online, a smart, competitive intelligence strategy can be accomplished with a few keystrokes and no out-of-pocket expenses. Your only cost is the amount of time it takes to do the research.

Now it's time to take off your foggles and research your competitors, and, in doing so, gain a deep appreciation for some external reference points. We'll essentially use the same formatted worksheets that you filled out for your internal assessment to study your competitors.

The first step is to decide on your competitive set. Since we should always strive to improve our business, your first focus should be on businesses you feel are the top in their field. If you're a shop owner, what other stores like yours, on your town's main street or in the next town over, are thriving? If you're having trouble coming up with a list of highly respected competitors, then expand your focus geographically and think in a five-, ten-, or twenty-mile radius. Try to come up with a list of at least five other businesses similar to yours that are as successful as, and preferably more successful than, your own.

With your short list of competitors, do a first pass of their on-line reviews. To get the greatest cross-section of online reviews, go beyond just one review site, like Yelp, and read reviews on any other review sites that cater to your type of business. During the first pass, narrow your analysis to the last twelve months of reviews for each business.

A great business practice that you can start during this analysis is to constantly review and revise the vision that you have for your business, and, if necessary, modify that vision based on what's happening in the marketplace. As you begin the practice of con-ducting periodic competitive analysis, the goal is not only to find competitors who are gaining market share in your industry but also to measure the ways the market itself is changing and how you plan to adapt, keeping in mind that you have to do so while staying genuine to where you want to take your business.

As you read your competitors' reviews, ask yourself if there are elements to your own vision that are lacking. For example, if you are a toy manufacturer, analyzing your competitive posi-tioning by reading consumer reviews of toys similar to those that you make, you might discover that what you thought was a unique offering has been fulfilled by your competition. Con-versely, as you read through competitors' reviews you might find that there's a gap in the marketplace in serving an unmet need. Are there overall positive or negative trends that you've noticed? Jot down those trends for each competitor. As you're going through the first pass, ask yourself how your own business sets itself apart from your competitors. Is there something that dif-ferentiates you? Is there a reason why a customer would choose to patronize your business versus a competitor's?

For each of your competitors, review their Web site, marketing messages, and any materials that they've posted on their review page. Can you get a sense of what the vision for their business is? Write down your impressions for each of your competitors, along with any overall positive or negative trends in their reviews. Now you're ready for a more in-depth pass at their reviews.

Going through each of your competitors, apply the review criteria that you used for your business, noting the positives and negatives for each. At the bottom of each page note any additional criteria that came to you as you read the reviews that might be areas you've missed in your own business.

Once completed, given everything you've read about the way consumers view your business and the way they view your competitors, ask yourself why someone would choose to visit your business versus your competitors. If you're having trouble answering that question, it might be time to revisit your vision.

Are your competitors true to their own vision? Did their reviews match their marketing claims on their Web site, or what they submitted on their review page? Based on what you read, and any changes that you made to your own vision statement, perhaps you should modify what you share through your own marketing materials. Is there a deficiency in the marketplace that you can capitalize on?

As you think about the transparency of your competitive set, remember to constantly be on the lookout for a market inefficiency. As you review competitors, have you found any whose overall ratings are not commensurate with how busy or profitable their businesses appear to be?

When you find the scenario of a store, restaurant, product, or brand that has horrible reviews but appears to have a very strong business, you have identified an opportunity to exploit a marketing inefficiency. Taking advantage of that situation could be as simple as changing your marketing message to address where a competitor is lacking. Perhaps my vision is to create an organic café but also provide friendly, efficient service, something that, based on reviews, is completely lacking. These types of adjustments that take advantage of a competitor's shortcomings demonstrate how we can focus and improve our business with laser precision.

As you read through your competitors' best reviews, ask yourself, what did my competitor do to earn praise from their customer? Did you notice any mentions in your competitors' reviews that might give insight into their success in being memorable? While I don't suggest copying your competitor's signature items or service (assuming she/he has one), you should use their five-star reviews and mentions of unexpected positive experiences as a springboard to finding your opportunity to be memorable.

Study a Failure

As philosopher George Santayana stated, "Those who cannot remember the past are condemned to repeat it." That lesson is specifically applicable to this practice of online review competitive analysis. Along with analyzing your competitors who are thriving, you should think about doing a postmortem analysis on businesses in your sector that didn't make it.

Fresh Choice, a California-based all-you-can-eat salad bar chain that provided fresh, healthy foods, once had fifty-eight different locations throughout California, Texas, and Washington. I can remember my first visit to a Fresh Choice when I moved to northern California in 1993. Tucked away in the back of Stanford Mall, the self-service salad bar was filled with diners mostly in their twenties.

When I was a new California resident, this eatery represented everything I thought California to be—bright, healthy, bountiful. Over the years the chain's success started to dwindle. The twentysomethings started to disappear, and were replaced by older, more cost-conscious diners attracted by the chain's all-you-can-eat offering.

The demise was predictable. If you read through the Yelp reviews for the few locations that remained before the company filed Chapter 7 in 2012, you could reconstruct what went wrong. Let's apply the first step of our analysis to the demise of Fresh Choice.

Fresh Choice displayed their value statements in the dining room of every outlet:

1. We act guest first

2. We have great food

3. We are clean

4. We hire the best and we take care of them

Compare those four pillars of the Fresh Choice value statement to how consumers perceived their restaurant in my hometown of

San Mateo, California (at the time it closed, the restaurant had eighty-seven reviews, for an aggregate rating of two and a half stars, on Yelp).

C.F., a Yelp Elite reviewer, writes in her one-star review:

> Should have known when on my last visit, two of the three specialty salad choices were plain romaine lettuce. They had duplicates of many salad topping options and all the signs were lined up incorrectly. When brought up to the cashier, they just shrugged and said, "Yeah, it's been like that for a while."

From reviewer A.H.:

> No eggs, no pizza, no muffins, no potato, no Chinese noodle salad and with few empty trays!! They do have fruit flies flying around the watermelons. I ask for the manager and waited for half-hour and no one bother to come out and speak with me.

> Fresh choice used to be very good but not anymore and we all know why. . . . Will not go there anymore.

Or this review from Patrick G.:

> A lousy choice. The salad bar had no cheese. My wife wanted real butter on her baked potato, and the manager told her that they only carried margarine. The food was pretty lousy, and that's even considering the low expecta-

tions that you have for an all you can eat place. This place would get 1 star but for the fact that it is a dirt cheap place to take toddlers (2 and under eat free and kids 3–5 eat for a $1.99), and they don't seem to mind the lousy food.

It's clear from the negative reviews that along the way Fresh Choice failed to live up to each of its four value statements. According to David Boyd, the former president of Fresh Choice, who is in the process of reinventing the chain as California Fresh, "the 20–30 somethings that work at Google, they're not coming to eat at our place."[1]

Reconstructing the demise, Mr. Boyd has a point here. The marketplace for twenty- to thirtysomethings has changed in the last fifteen years. The trajectory of Fresh Choice went from a farm-fresh–to–table vision to an all-you-can-eat, low-cost buffet that catered to an older, deal-savvy crowd.

Fresh Choice was probably forced to skimp on quality, of both the food and the staff, to make margins. Values 2 and 4 fell by the wayside. If you're hiring the lowest-cost labor and are probably running a much leaner crew, it's consequently hard to put the customer first and keep your restaurants clean. Given the turmoil, it becomes impossible to act "guest first," as was evident in the reviewers' interactions with the San Mateo restaurant's staff.

Could Fresh Choice's impending doom have been avoided with some competitive intelligence? Possibly. What advice would you give to David Boyd as he attempts to relaunch the chain as California Fresh?

Based on what I've covered in this chapter, I would suggest

that Boyd come up with a new concept, then reimagine his vision and value statements. Next, he should figure out what restaurants are part of his competitive set. Last, rather than navigate blindly, or with foggles, he should go through the competitive user review exercise to figure out what's working (and not working) in concepts close to his vision for California Fresh.

Now Study a Success

James Peo and his wife, Jade, founded Veo Optics in San Francisco in 2009, and have grown their operation to five stores spread throughout the city. Their first store was so successful, the fire department required that they post an employee at the door to ensure that they didn't exceed the store's maximum capacity of people. When was the last time you saw crowd control at an eyeglass store?

I sit down with James in his newest store in the One California building, close to the Embarcadero waterfront in downtown San Francsico. The store is immaculate, and James immediately asks if he can see my eyeglasses. "Great choice," he says as he hands them back to me with an approving nod. James is dressed to the nines, wearing a sports coat and vest. He bills himself on the Veo Web site as the founder and celebrity stylist.

We talk about how Veo Optics differentiates itself from the crowded field of eyewear stores in the Bay Area. James tells me about the history of eyeglass shops in California, and how the lobbyists for the medical community have created an unfair advantage for optometrists (ODs) and ophthalmologists (MDs). Both an OD and an MD are allowed to sell eyeglasses in their practice, as well as open a retail storefront and provide eye exams. While an OD or MD can hire an optician in the state of California, an optician who has opened their own eyeglass store cannot hire an OD or MD to provide a full-service shop. According to James, optometrists successfully lobbied the California legislature to pass a law that gives ODs and MDs competitive advantage when it comes to selling eyewear. While this competitive advantage might be nice for doctors, the restriction in free trade has hampered competition, and as a result has led to a decline in quality of service. James compares California's lack of competition to New York, where there are no laws regarding opticians hiring optometrists. "In New York you have the crème de la crème of eyeglass stores. Many of them are owned by opticians that employ MDs and ODs." Because of the fierce competition they have to bring their best.

When James opened Veo in 2009, he did so knowing that California legislation had caused inefficiency in the marketplace. The majority of eyeglass stores in California are within doctors' offices; they're side businesses with lackluster selections and service that is in line with what one usually experiences in a doctor's office. By surveying the marketplace through online reviews, he realized that if he was going to open a store without an OD or MD, he had to differentiate his store to compensate for the patient's inconvenience of having to visit a doctor's office before purchasing glasses in his store.

While the legal battles continued, James felt that he could best the larger national chains by providing superior service. The niche that he found was providing a good selection of higher-end eyewear, and also providing customers with a stylist to make specific frame recommendations based on the customer's facial structure. On his Web site, James features before and after pictures of customers who have been fitted with eyeglasses more appropriate for their facial features. He also has a prominent tab at the top of his Web site that features his Yelp reviews for all five stores. It's evident that James, along with being stylish and driven by his convictions, is someone who starts with the end point in mind.

Online review sites such as Yelp serve multiple purposes for Veo. By reviewing the ratings for other eyeglass stores in the area, James substantiated his observation that there was inefficiency in the market for superior service when purchasing eyewear. James admits that he still reads his competitors' reviews on a nightly basis. "I want to learn everything I can about how I can provide superior service compared to any other competitor."

Online reviews are also a channel for James to reinforce his marketing message that Veo is a higher-end provider of glasses that are selected through a consultative appointment with a stylist. According to James, Yelp was instrumental in the opening of his first store in 2009, which received 209 five-star reviews almost immediately. James confides that online reviews can have a massive impact on revenue and that Yelp is Veo's most significant channel for the acquisition of new customers. When his store does get negative reviews, though those reviews are usually filtered, if they do manage to drop the overall ranking, it can have a serious impact on revenue.

James's hyperfocus on Yelp has also made him acutely aware of the importance of superior service. He says he trains his staff to "underpromise and overdeliver" and explains the importance of constantly exceeding his customers' expectations. For example, if a pair of glasses is expected to be ready for the customer in a week's time, his staff will say that it usually takes a little longer, so that when the store calls the customer earlier than expected, he's pleasantly surprised. James also emphasizes that superior service is not limited to his customers; it's imperative that anyone entering his store, customer or not, experiences exceptional hospitality. "If someone comes in needing directions, we'll go out of our way to help them find where they're going. If someone needs change for a meter, we have change. If a tourist comes in with broken glasses, even though we'll never see them again, we go out of our way to repair their glasses, clean them, adjust them." James is reinforcing that excellent customer service is a daily practice that is inclusive of anyone who enters his shop.

Along with the value of online reviews to drive business, the most important lesson that we can take away from Veo Optics is the power of competitive intelligence. Competitive intelligence is not a static exercise. As you turn to online reviews to help better your business, you'll quickly realize that the number of reviews, the feedback, and trending, or monitoring the change in average reviews for yourself and your competitive set, are very dynamic. It's clear that when James launched Veo in 2009 he had the end point in mind. What James has demonstrated, however, is the importance of using online reviews as a competitive intelligence to validate that your end point fulfills a need in the marketplace that is currently unfulfilled. Instead of focusing so much on your own online reviews, you could learn a lot from the way that James approaches the wealth of information that's contained in the reviews of his competitors.

Now it's time for our next exercise. Like James, we need to survey our competitive set to discover if there are any inefficiencies or opportunities in the marketplace. If you're in the service business, is there a lack of quality customer service? If you sell electronics, is there an unmet demand for specific types of gadgets? Start by making a list of every business in your area that you consider competitive. Now for each competitor start a new page with two columns, one for positive reviews and one for negative. First start with your competitor's positive five-star reviews. As you read each review, are there similarities between their customers' praise and your vision? You should ask yourself while reading the most positive reviews for your competitors, is the vision that I have for my business really unique, does it set my business apart? Now read your competitors' negative reviews. Make note of any common themes that you notice in the one- and two-star reviews for your competitive set.

When you've finished compiling the negative feedback (I'm sure you enjoyed this exercise much more than reviewing your own negative reviews), were you able to find any unmet or unserved needs? If you were, consider ways that your business could fill those gaps. If, and only if, you can serve an unmet need you've discovered in this exercise and stay true to your vision, it's time to amend your end point and best your competition.

Organic Food and the Elasticity of Demand

Walking in our neighborhood, I find it remarkable that one particular restaurant is packed every lunch and dinner service every day of the week. Given how busy it is, you might think that the café has great reviews, but the restaurant has amassed fifty-three reviews since opening in 2013 and has an average review rating of two and a half stars on Yelp. Currently, this café in Burlingame is one of the worst-reviewed restaurants on the peninsula, yet there's a wait for a table every day of the week.

To explain this decoupling of overall stars and filled tables, you have to understand the concept of elasticity of demand. There are certain things in life that consumers are willing to pay for, even if the price of those products exceeds other similar products. A good example of an inelastic demand service would be your local emergency room. If you're having a heart attack and find yourself in a hospital emergency room, you are willing to avail yourself of the staff's assistance regardless of how much will be charged or, if you're insured, how much of your deductible will be affected. In a suburban neighborhood where *gluten* is a dirty word, the opening of a café that serves only organic food creates an inelastic demand curve.

One of the key functions of online reviews for consumers is to diminish uncertainty by providing mass opinion about an unknown vendor. Because of that additional data, independent businesses experience an increase in demand elasticity. In his study of restaurants in Seattle, Washington, and the effects of Yelp star ratings on revenue, Harvard's Michael Luca found that the 5 to 9 percent lift in restaurant revenue per star was limited to independent restaurants. Chain restaurants or those restaurants affiliated with a national brand were not as affected by variations in Yelp star ratings. As consumers become more reliant on online reviews, the decision to visit a business becomes more dependent on the aggregate reviews for that business. Businesses that are affiliated with national chains are the one exception to that observation, as they have more review-based elasticity. That elasticity is rooted in an advantage that chain restaurants have when it comes to the strength of their brand. According to Luca, "because chains already have little uncertainty about quality their demand does not respond to consumer reviews."[2]

The brand advantage that a McDonald's, Olive Garden, or Cheesecake Factory has over the local eatery is eroding over time, though. While reviews aren't affecting chain restaurant revenue, there is a tectonic shift from national branded eateries to local establishments. According to Luca, when analyzing national chain restaurants' pre- and post-online-review popularity, there is a tradeoff in revenue, with independents cannibalizing the revenue from national chains. Yet with only a handful of restaurants in the Bay Area, the café hardly qualifies as a national chain, so there must be another reason for its review-inelastic demand.

How can one of the worst-reviewed businesses in my hometown be one of the busiest? Scanning through the reviews, they trend both on bad food as well as on poor service. Take the dining summary offered by N.A. on Yelp:

> This was the worst meal I have had in years. If it was possible to give no stars I would. 1st we had a very annoying waiter . . . who we dubbed the screen saver. He probably asked us if everything was ok about 30 times (not kidding) over our dinner. When we did complain he pretended he could not hear us. The ambiance was tight and

you could tell the people working there were very awkward. [He] did not read us the dinner specials so we missed out on other entrees. (which was a good thing in the end.) Our table was a giant see-saw that wobbled so much that I could lean on it and my friends water would slide to my side. They said they were dealing with "growing pains" when we complained. Nobody fixed it.

Having eaten at both the restaurant and their small side-door café, I would have to agree with N.A.'s assessment as well as the others that have bestowed one or two stars on the place. G.F.G. writes:

We ordered 2 gluten free pizzas, the beet salad and 2 orders of the coconut halibut. The gluten free pizzas were nothing special and pretty dry. The salad was great. Both orders of fish were really dry and overcooked so we sent them back. When they redid them, they were cooked correctly but you could definitely tell they were using frozen fish—it had that frozen fish consistency. Charging $23 for frozen fish is unacceptable.

There is one thing that sets the café apart from every other restaurant on the street, or in the city, for that matter. Analyzing the psychographic makeup of the communities surrounding the restaurant confirms my hunch that this particular restaurant has created a more elastic demand by catering to the specific needs of its community, and by being the only restaurant for miles to do so. The restaurant bills itself as a "café organic," with all organic produce, free-range organic poultry, and sustainable seafood. The menu even offers the latest in dieting trends, "the cleanse," a liquid-based diet of fruit and vegetable juices meant to detox the body.

According to the Experian Mosaic segmentation system, which groups the U.S. consumer into seventy-three different psychographic types based on geography, the most predominant segment in the café's community is what they term A01: American Royalty, the most affluent segment, with household income more than $250,000 per year.[3] This group is more likely to belong to a gym (nearly three times more likely than the American public), more likely to eat healthy snacks, and more likely than the population to buy and eat organic food.

In the world of online reviews, elasticity of demand is not only the function of brand but can also be created by fulfilling an unmet need in the community. The takeaway for businesses is, in the process of doing this assessment as well as your competitive assessment, as you survey businesses in your neighborhood and field, be on the lookout for an inherent inefficiency in the marketplace. Is there a business whose reviews appear to be out of sync with their business success? If you are able to find one of these gems in your community, the next question to ask yourself is, why is this business busy despite its reviews? Are they doing something that distinguishes them from surrounding businesses? If you can identity what that is, and if it fits within the vision for your business, by replicating what that business is doing and adding quality of product and service, you will be able to exploit an inefficiency in the marketplace.

The café will probably be busy for the foreseeable future, but over time, as the marketplace finds and solves for inefficiencies, they'll have to improve their food and service or abdicate their monopoly of organic food on the peninsula. While negative reviews can harm some businesses and have no effect on others, it might surprise you to know that for some businesses, negative reviews can actually help.

Some Negative Reviews Can Be Good for You

While it's been shown that there is a positive correlation between reviews and revenue (at least in the case of restaurants), research demonstrates that some negative reviews for a business can actually be beneficial.

According to a research study conducted by UK software company Reevoo, consumers actively seek out negative reviews. In fact, according to the study, negative reviews are the most popular on product Web sites, surpassing most-recent reviews or reviews from "people like me." The study also finds that consumers spend four times as long on sites when they read bad reviews, and purchase 67 percent more than the population as a whole. The study also found that 68 percent of consumers trust the reviews that they read when they see both good and bad reviews for a business or product.[4] Conversely, the study also found that 95 percent of consumers suspect censorship or faked reviews when they don't see any bad reviews for a business.[5]

According to research from New York University, it's not just the negative star rating that affects the sale of goods online.

NYU professor Panagiotis Ipeirotis studied the effects of positive and negative reviews on Amazon resellers. He wanted to find out why some customers chose to buy a Canon EOS 7D camera from one retailer, Willoughby's, at a higher price versus buying the exact same camera from another retailer, 17th Street Photo, at a lower price; it was a 7 percent price difference, of $140 off $1,999. The data shows that certain negative phrases tend to push up conversion rates.[6]

In analyzing thousands of transactions on Amazon for this camera, Ipeirotis's research showed that online reputation translates to the ability of high-rated resellers to charge a premium for their products. His research quantifies the value of a positive online reputation. When Ipeirotis analyzed the text of reseller reviews, some terms within positive reviews had a positive effect on the reseller's reputation while others had a negative effect. For example, when analyzing the electronic resellers selling the Canon camera, comments such as "wonderful experience" or "outstanding seller" translated to a $5.86 and $5.76 premium that the reseller could charge, respectively. Negative comments such as "never received" or "defective product" resulted in a deduction of $7.56 and $6.82 from what that vendor could charge, respectively.[7]

His research then took an interesting twist. Some positive comments actually resulted in a deduction in what price a specific product could command from an online retailer. "Best Camera," for example, resulted in a drop of value of −0.2 percent, while negative statements such as "[this camera has] video problems with some SDHC cards" had a positive effect on sales for that camera.[8] How could negative comments in reviews actually increase the value of a product? Ipeirotis's thinking is that vague positive comments leave the purchaser thinking there is nothing specifically positive that the reviewer can say, therefore the product must not be any good. Conversely, when there are specific negative comments, the reader tends to believe the reviewer. If the complaint doesn't highlight a deal breaker, it can translate into increased sales.

As an award-winning chef, Craig Stoll's repulsion to negative reviews is understandable. What's counterintuitive and what should change Stoll's mind about negative reviews is that they're actually valuable in lending overall credibility to a business's review page. However, not all negative reviews are created equal. Factors such as phrases used and grammar and spelling can have a big effect. When Ipeirotis looked into grammar and spelling mistakes in online travel reviews on TripAdvisor, he found that errors on positive reviews can decrease the percentage of online bookings while good grammar and spelling on negative reviews can increase a hotel's bookings.[9] Applying Ipeirotis's previous findings, as long as the negative reviews are for smaller, peripheral issues, negative reviews lift sales.

While Ipeirotis was on the speaking circuit discussing his findings, online retailer Zappos hired editors via Amazon's Mechanical Turk to correct grammar and spelling errors in customer reviews posted on the site, resulting in an increase in overall revenue.[10]

In a separate research project, professors Jonah Berger and Alan Sorensen found that negative critical (or professional) reviews could have a positive effect on book sales.[11] Supporting the notion that any press is good press, Berger and his colleagues looked at the sales of 244 hardcover titles that were also reviewed by the *New York Times*. What they found regarding positive reviews was not surprising. A positive review for a book generated between a 32 and a 52 percent increase in demand. Where the results of their research take an interesting turn is when they looked at negative critical reviews in the *New York Times*. In the case of established authors, a negative review could reduce demand for the panned book by 15 percent, but when an author was an unknown, a negative review could increase that book's sales by up to 45 percent.[12]

Why You Need Product Reviews on Your Site

Shortly after Amazon launched in 1995, the company's first employee, Shel Kaphan, added online reviews to its Web site, pioneering the idea of an online retailer posting consumer-generated opinions right on the page where a buyer could complete a purchase. Unbeknownst to many, Amazon employees were responsible for writing the first reviews themselves, effectively seeding the site with enough consumer-generated content to give the idea a push. Founder Jeff Bezos believed that if the site had more consumer-generated reviews for books than any other retailer, then Amazon would have a huge advantage.[13]

Down the coast in San Jose, California, I was working at Dataquest. "They must be crazy" was the common consensus, as a number of analysts gathered in the hallway of the Dataquest offices. Dataquest, later acquired by the Gartner Group, was one of the premier analyst organizations covering tech. It was already a stretch to think that an online retailer could sell books, sight unseen, given the tactile advantage that a bricks-and-mortar bookstore had. But to put people's reviews on the same page where you're trying to sell something seemed like retailer suicide. "What if a product got all bad reviews, nobody is going to buy it," one analyst surmised. "Vendors will probably pull out once they get wind of this, nobody wants to give that kind of power to consumers."

In retrospect, Bezos was onto something. While publishing consumer reviews on products would surely dampen sales for those that were rated negatively, overall for the entire site, the addition of reviews accomplished a couple of objectives. First, and most important, was the establishment of trust between an online store and the consumer. In the mid-nineties, trust in a virtual store was a precious commodity. The other invaluable asset that Bezos acquired when Amazon launched reviews was the addition of a community to the site, a community that encouraged engagement. Fast-forward to 2013, and almost every medium to large business has online reviews built into their site. Small businesses are joining as well, using off-the-shelf software and Web site plug-ins to provide review capabilities to their sites.

Do you ever wonder why so many retailers send out e-mails and populate checkout pages with requests for you to review products on their site? It's in the numbers. According to social commerce firm Reevoo, having fifty or more reviews for a product on your site can translate to a 4.6 percent increase in sales for that item.[14] According to iPerceptions, 63 percent of consumers are more likely to make a purchase on a site that has user reviews.[15]

The evidence is overwhelming for placing reviews on a page, yet a few retailers are still pushing back on the idea. What reason do they give? Are they worried their products will get bad reviews or their sales will suffer? Those retailers that don't have reviews on their site should have another fear—customers churning off their site to find an online store that does provide sufficient user reviews. Using Experian Marketing Services data, I analyzed a category of Web sites that have online reviews and compared it to a category of Web sites that don't have online reviews. To measure the risk of churning customers, I looked at where Internet users went after visiting each retailer category. For those sites that had reviews, 33.4 percent visited another online retailer immediately after visiting the subject retailer. For those sites that did not have reviews, that percentage rose to 47.9 percent. Since more than 70 percent of consumers consult online reviews before making their purchase decisions, if you've chosen not to have reviews on your site, you're likely sending your customers to Amazon or another major online retailer to check reviews, and while they happen to be at your competitor's site, they may just decide to buy there. While some will always be stuck in pre-Amazon thinking, retailers that have a hope of surviving this challenging economy are those that realize the value of trust, community, and increased conversion.

For the small businesses that don't sell products, consider installing a widget, or plug-in for your Web site that will pull reviews on your business from popular sites. Widgets are available from Yelp, TripAdvisor, Google Places for Business, and others.

In recent years, putting reviews on your own site has become in vogue for the hotel industry as well. On the booking page of a Wyndham hotel there is a feed of TripAdvisor reviews for every one of their properties next to the hotel rates. The feed doesn't discriminate; it doesn't just show positive reviews. The Four Seasons also has a TripAdvisor icon on its page, and a link on every reservation page to check the online reviews for that specific property. There's an interesting by-product to becoming so transparent with your reviews. For example, the GM of every Wyndham hotel knows that there are no secrets; his or her property's rating is there for everyone to see. This level of transparency fosters a desire to constantly improve one's property's rating. From the corporate boardroom to the individual hotel staff meeting, everyone is becoming hyperaware of their online reviews.

Hopefully, I've provided you with enough data to help you through the process of accepting your negative reviews. Of course there is one possible case that we're ignoring. A very small percentage of people reading this book may actually have a business that warrants a barrage of critical one-star reviews.

6

Do This for Great Reviews

* * * * *

As the cold drizzle turns into a steady rain outside Paddington Station, I lean into the passenger window of the black London taxi. "Do you know how to get to the Hotel 41?" The cabbie looks at me with some confusion. Known for their encyclopedic knowledge of city streets, restaurants, and hotels, London taxi drivers are rarely stumped. "It's connected to The Rubens Hotel," I add as an additional clue. A look of recognition and relief flashes across the cabbie's face. I open the door and hoist my luggage into the backseat of the black cab, eager to get to the hotel and check in after a long transatlantic flight.

Having stayed at the hotel on my previous five visits to London, I'm not surprised that the driver doesn't know of the property. In fact, not one cabbie from my earlier visits had heard of the hotel. If you weren't specifically looking for the Hotel 41, there's a good chance you would never know it existed—that is, unless you rely on consumer reviews when booking travel arrangements.

Hidden on the fifth floor of its sister hotel, The Rubens, in the fashionable Belgravia neighborhood, this small, thirty-room boutique hotel with rooms nearly half the price of legendary five-star properties such as The Savoy, The Langham, and The Dorchester, has accomplished one thing that those other luxury properties have found elusive. Over the course of the last two years, it's maintained top-ranking status on TripAdvisor for hotels in London, besting 1,076 other properties while at the same time remaining London's best-kept secret. In fact, the Red Carnation hotel chain, owners of the Hotel 41, currently holds the top three positions on TripAdvisor, with the Milestone and Egerton House Hotel vying for the number-one spot.

Red Carnation's management and staff aren't the product of an award-winning customer service excellence training program. At the 41 there's no pool, gym, or grand lobby, and the room sizes are on the small side, even for London. With rooms that range between three hundred and six hundred euros per night, their rates are well below the prices commanded by other five-star hotels, but 41's ranking is probably not based on value.

Most of the 41's previous guests would have little trouble identifying how they've maintained their top rank—they would point to the staff's near fanatical obsession with guest satisfaction and online consumer reviews. "We all have TripAdvisor set as the home page on our smartphones," admits one of the hotel managers. "We're constantly checking our ranking and looking for new reviews." "We had four reviews last week," the resident manager chimes in.

Like many other travelers, I found the Hotel 41 via the online review site TripAdvisor. Based on 1,380 reviews, with a five-star average and reviewer comments such as "the best service I have ever experienced," "Shh—keep it a secret," and "Can I live here? I can't wait to return," my mind was at ease that I would be comfortable during my brief business trip.

After being escorted to the hotel's atrium library, I feel like I have entered the wood-paneled library of an old-money English family. The two lit fireplaces on opposite ends of the room radiate warmth as other guests relax over breakfast and the morning newspaper. A few hotel staff cluster around an executive wood desk. I drop my bags and sit in the cushy leather high-back chair opposite Magda, the front-desk manager. Without prompting, the staff remembers my visit from a year prior, and a skim latte and biscuits arrive from the kitchen. This is remarkable because up to this point I haven't yet uttered a word. I cup the warm coffee mug in my hands, which helps diminish my chill from the dreary weather outside; Magda quickly handles the hotel check-in. The other staff politely inquire as to my plans during this short visit, and offer to make reservations, suggestions, or do anything to make my stay more pleasurable.

Unpacking from my flight, I become acutely aware that the hotel's staff, through obsessive attention to satisfaction and reviews, had harnessed the power of consumer-generated opinions. Rather than spending significant money on branding campaigns, offering cut-rate pricing through hotel discount Web sites, or spending inordinate amounts of money on advertising, traditional or online, Hotel 41 has discovered that going the extra mile with hotel guests will likely result in excellent reviews on TripAdvisor, keeping the hotel at its top position in London, which in turn will lead to even more new guests who will discover this hidden hotel via online reviews.

As I think about Hotel 41's proactive approach to online reviews and its success in driving new reservations through TripAdvisor, one thing becomes very clear to me. What makes the Hotel 41 and other winners in the online review space unique is that they have mastered the application of established best practices in hospitality to this new mode of consumer research, decision making, and advocacy. For the most part, business rules haven't changed; what has changed is a rapid acceleration in technology that is changing how businesses and consumers behave. At the heart of every online review success story I've studied is a true passion on the part of business owners and their employees.

Online reviews, however, can be catastrophic for those businesses that are running on autopilot. In a world where consumers have a plethora of choices, the lack of passion becomes very evident as reviewers highlight every miss.

There's a third scenario between businesses that are passionate and those that aren't—the businesses that cater to the whims of online reviews and are missing a clear road map of what they want to be.

Rule 1: Passion Drives Positive Reviews

Early in my career I had the pleasure of working with a number of very promising start-ups. There was one big difference between the companies that made it and those that did not: a clear understanding of where the company was going and a detailed road map of how to get there.

It's no different from the mental steps you go through getting in your car each day. Each time you back out of your driveway, unless you're just going for a drive to kill time, there's a good chance that you know your end destination before you drive off. If you've never been to your day's destination, you probably entered the address into a GPS or have printed directions. If you have been there before, you know the path to take.

Now that you've decided to leverage reviews for your business, it's even more important that you have a clear vision of your end point and how you're going to get there. As you begin to rely on reviews for finding ways to improve your business, you'll find that it's far too easy to get off course as you try to satisfy every customer. The most important lesson you'll learn from this rule is that it's impossible to satisfy everyone. As we've learned from previous chapters, there will be some dissatisfied customers who will write bad reviews, and you'll have to be okay with that. One way you can provide yourself some peace of mind in this process is by being able to accept some bad reviews because the experience sought by the reviewer is outside your mission for your company.

There have been countless books written on mission and vision statements and specific goals that roll up to help us achieve our end point. Rather than rehash the best practices of writing a mission statement, let's focus on what your ultimate vision is for your business. It's time for another exercise, and this one is important.

Remove yourself, as best as you can, from all distractions. If you have an office, close the door. Turn off your phone and computer. Take a minute to relax, and think back to why you started your business. What was your vision when you first opened, or, if you work in a larger company, think about what dreams you had the first day you started on the job. Are you as excited today as you were when you started your venture? If yes, that's great, now it's time to push yourself even further; if not, it's time to reset and find a vision that you can be passionate about.

Now, with your competitive assessment in mind, ask yourself this question: what about my vision sets my business apart from everyone else's in my field? If your answer is "nothing," then it's time to dream bigger. One thing I've discovered in studying businesses that have unlocked the potential of online reviews is that the owners are all incredibly passionate about the product or service that they represent. James at Veo had a very strong vision of what he wanted to accomplish; it was with that conviction that he was able to execute and deliver a standout shop in a field saturated with competitors. The staff at Hotel 41 and the other two Red Carnation properties in London had a red booklet written by the chain's founder describing her vision. The secret to delivering on your passion is to make the end point of what you want your business to be as vivid as possible.

When you've found the vision for your business or product, take out another piece of paper or open your laptop computer or tablet and write out a narrative. Write a story from your customer's perspective. What is it like to walk into your business or use your product for the first time? Be as specific as possible. If you run a café, imagine how the customers feel as they're greeted when they walk into your shop. Write about how welcoming your café feels, and what specifically keeps your customers coming back every morning on their way into the office. Maybe mention the fact that the customer who frequents your shop and orders the same espresso drink every morning is delighted to find that you had already started his drink when you saw him pull his car into the parking lot. Perhaps you'll write about how you differentiate your business from the chain coffee places by knowing your customers by name, taking an interest in their weekend, or asking how their kid's soccer game turned out. If you're a hotel proprietor, think about how your guests' every concern is addressed even before they mention it, or how you've drawn guests out of their rooms to interact with staff so that they feel an emotional connection to your hotel. This simple exercise of defining your end point will provide you with the framework that you'll need to assess every positive and negative review you receive.

Passion Drives Mission

Along with having the end point in mind, it's also critically important that you are genuine to your vision and that you have the passion to get from point A to point B. When considering reviewers from Yelp, TripAdvisor, Angie's List, and others, it's clear that having a passion to deliver an excellent product or service is very discernible to the customer, and that those customers who benefit from your passion are most likely to write a five-star review for your business.

If you look on the jacket of this book you'll see that Misti Layne was the photographer who took my headshot. I first encountered Misti while working at a San Francisco–based search engine in 2003. I was recruiting small business owners to participate in a focus group for a new product that we were launching. The first thing that struck me about Misti was the passion she had for her photography business.

"I can't do anything else. I have to do photography, there's no other choice for me. I don't want to go back working in a cubicle. I want to do a good job. It's my pride, my honor, and my duty if you hire me," Misti Layne said. She's been shooting weddings, engagements, and headshots full-time for the last ten years, and is one of the highest-rated San Francisco photographers on Yelp, with fifty-five five-star reviews. The passion that Misti has for photography is unmistakable. She took my headshots for my last book. I thought she'd be an excellent source to tell me how she's managed to be one of the top five-star-rated photographers in a city with thousands in her profession.

Along with being a highly rated photographer, Misti was also an Elite Yelper from 2005 to 2008, with more than 560 reviews. While Misti might be considered an outlier, she is also a perfect example of the first rule of getting great reviews online: have your end point in mind and be genuine to that vision. As I talk to her about her business, it's clear that she has an unwavering passion to deliver the best possible experience for her customers. "I love waking up in the morning knowing that I am going to take a picture of something, anything," she writes on her blog, and she firmly believes that as long as the end product is excellent, she will receive outstanding reviews.

I ask her what her secret is to getting five-star reviews. As a rule, she doesn't ask clients for reviews. In her opinion doing so would probably result in a filtered review (removal by Yelp's algorithm as a possibly fraudulent review). The reason that many business-requested reviews show up in filtered results, largely unread by the public, is that the reviewer is a first-time reviewer without any history and therefore disadvantaged in the filtering algorithm. She goes on to explain that she doesn't find a five-star review to be something exceptional; rather, she says, "When someone gives me five stars, it's confirmation to me that I'm doing my job. Whatever it takes, I'm going to do a good job."

As we discussed in chapter 3, bad reviews can often lead business owners to disregard or ignore the online review channel completely. A passionate commitment to your mission can go a long way in helping you come to terms with negative opinions of your business. One corporate executive who left his lucrative career to pursue his passion of building the perfect barbershop did just that in a very unorthodox way.

Passion and the Counterintuitive World of Reviews

Before telling you this next story, I caution you not to try this at home (or the office), unless your business fits the style of mischievous marketing invented by Matthew Berman, also known as Mohawk Matt.

Matt left his career as a global marketing executive for Procter & Gamble in 2008 to pursue his lifelong dream of owning and running a barbershop. After spending eight months in barber college, Matt opened Bolt Barbers, an edgy shop that endeavors to re-create the barbershop experience. Customers are treated to extras along with their haircut, such as several big screen TVs, and free Pabst Blue Ribbon beer (or PBR) for members of the Hairy Beasts Club (membership in the club can be had for a nominal fee and includes a laminated card in the shape of a blade). The space housing Bolt Barbers' downtown L.A. shop exudes a cool vibe, part industrial space, part garage, complete with a large sign hanging from the ceiling that reads, PEOPLE HATE US ON YELP.

In some ways Matt wanted to resurrect that old barbershop of the past, while at the same time providing a cool, hip atmosphere that would appeal to white- and blue-collar workers in downtown Los Angeles. In assembling the space, Matt located a regulation twenty-two-foot shuffleboard table. Unfortunately, the table had been in storage in Portland, Oregon, for more than six years and was in disrepair and out of balance. The only guy who could balance these tables on the West Coast was not available because he had just had knee surgery.

Within a few days of opening Bolt Barbers, the online reviews started to appear on Yelp. At first a few five-star reviews appeared after opening day, then Matt's shop received its first four-star review. Even though the review was overly positive, a less-than-perfect review got under Matt's skin. The reviewer enjoyed his haircut, liked everything about the experience, but docked the shop one star because the shuffleboard table wasn't level. In Matt's words, "I'm one of the only, no, probably the only, barbershop in the world that has a twenty-two-foot regulation shuffleboard table and here this guy is docking up a star because it's not level. Really!"

As the popularity of Bolt Barbers grew, so did the number of reviews. As with any business, Matt's shop received an occasional one-star review, and he began to realize that something he had learned about business when he was growing up wasn't true. As a kid, Matt worked at a grocery store with a sign above the door that read, RULE 1: THE CUSTOMER IS ALWAYS RIGHT, RULE 2: RE-READ RULE NUMBER 1. After Matt read a few of his one-star reviews he realized that "something I believed throughout business was no longer true. The customer wasn't always right, in fact, the customers that are wrong, thanks to social media, have a big megaphone to broadcast their opinion."

Rather than taking the traditional path of complaining about his negative reviews or, worse, ignoring online opinions entirely, Matt began printing out his one-star reviews, laminating them, and leaving them in the waiting area for customers to read. Matt quickly noticed that his customers loved reading the slams on his business. The laminated reviews went from the waiting-room table to the window of his new shop, and with that the "People Hate Us on Yelp" campaign was born. Matt's creative use of negative reviews became a viral success, leading to coverage in national magazines, newspapers, and broadcast television. Matt was getting unprecedented exposure for his new barbershop, including a Thrash Lab video produced by Ashton Kutcher. The PR stunt of capitalizing on his negative Yelp reviews was getting more coverage and engagement than any expensive advertising campaign could have mustered. He's opened a second location in West Hollywood, with a permanent metal sign affixed to the building declaring PEOPLE HATE US ON YELP, and is opening a Las Vegas location in a restored railroad car.

On the surface, Matt might be perceived as the ultimate antireview business owner; looking deeper into his business practices you'll see that he's the opposite. Matt's business, like so many others in downtown L.A., Hollywood, or any other town, is dependent on reviews to drive new business. Despite the fact that banners fly at all of his locations decrying "People Hate Us on Yelp," Matt's downtown location has a solid four stars. You would expect that Matt's campaign would not be very popular within the walls of Yelp's corporate offices, but Matt is actually on the small-business advisory council for Yelp.

Passion and commitment to mission also play important roles in the review space. Two of the most valuable by-products of online reviews are the internal and competitive intelligence that aggregate online opinions provide. If you skip the step of formulating a mission that you are passionate about, you bear the risk of making critical changes to your business solely to appease online reviewers. Matt's "People Hate Us on Yelp" campaign is a powerful demonstration that some online opinions are best disregarded. The key to Matt's ability to publicly deride some negative reviews while taking others seriously is that he measures each opinion against his passion and mission.

Rule 2: Build Power Through Transparency

With a solid vision, one of your most valuable tools to vault over the competition will be your willingness to embrace transparency. To prove that transparency can provide great opportunities to grow business, consider Jay Sofer, the owner of New York

City locksmith company Lockbusters. I first saw Jay on a You-Tube video sharing the stage with New York City mayor Michael Bloomberg at a Yelp event. Short in stature but full of energy, Jay couldn't wait to tell his rags-to-riches story.

In 2008, Jay was living in his mom's garage, broke and unemployed. Trying to make his way as a locksmith, his friends introduced him to building managers and supers in New York City to help him start his business, but his work was too sporadic. It was then that Jay stumbled onto online reviews. He noticed that the current players thrived on opacity. It was hard to tell what you were going to be charged when the locksmith would show up; the perception of the consumer as portrayed in reviews was that locksmiths were anything but transparent. Locksmithing in New York is a perfect example of the lack of transparency in business.

Brooklyn, specifically, appeared to be a market riddled with unscrupulous locksmiths. Many businesses still have one-star reviews, with comments about locksmiths arriving late, or, as Chloe S. wrote, "my neighbor was quoted a cheap price to get back into her apartment and these guys charged over $1300." Jay decided that he would differentiate himself from the existing businesses by being as transparent as possible. He started with pricing, and with the observation that the customer, locked out of his apartment late at night, is in a very poor position and at the mercy of that locksmith he found with a quick Google search. According to Jay, the locksmith business in New York City can be sketchy, and the last thing a person wants when he's locked out of his apartment is to deal with a service person who might scam him out of money with bogus fees. Jay's answer to differentiating himself is being on time, trustworthy, and courteous.

Jay's site lists prices ranging from $159 for an evening or weekend lockout to $99 for a daytime lockout. "With review sites, I have a whole page that allows me to be transparent. I put up a link to my page with all of my prices, there's no hidden fees and nothing to hide," he adds. In just six months, he became the highest-rated locksmith service on Yelp and Angie's List. More important, Jay says that almost all his business comes from online reviews. While he is a paid advertiser on Yelp, he doesn't engage in any other forms of advertising. He tried buying keywords on Google, but found that the online review business was more targeted and resulted in a far greater return on investment.

Transparency also helped Jay's business from a competitive perspective. "I love the fact that I'm held accountable for every little thing that I do. I know that my competition is held accountable as well, and my competition sucks." A big part of his "formula" for success is having common courtesy. Going to a call clean shaven, not smelling like a brewery or cigarette smoke, and being courteous to his clients puts him at an advantage compared to other New York locksmiths. Jay dresses and acts like he's going to meet his new girlfriend's parents. "Part of my formula for success is just presentation. In my industry just showing up on time and being presentable is totally unexpected." In the locksmith industry, that's enough for a five-star review.

In addition to his Yelp reviews, Jay has two Super Service Awards from Angie's List. Jay tells me, "When I get a client from Angie's List I know that they're my parents' age." Maximizing a review on Angie's List is all about being superprofessional and going the extra step in terms of being clean. Jay will put booties on his feet and prepares as though he's going to his grandparents' house. Transparency clearly means more to Jay than just posting pricing to his page. For Jay, transparency is a two-way street. He willingly and eagerly makes changes to his business practices from the feedback that he gets online. Jay also openly admits to the occasional one-star review screwup.

One recent bad review, Jay recalls, resulted from a call that came when he had been up working all night and, uncharacteristically, showed up late. The customer was sitting on the stoop and immediately mentioned to him that he was an active Yelper and intended to post a review of his service. Jay took this as a threat, i.e., if you don't do a good job, I'll be sure to give you a negative review. From there the job went from bad to worse. Jay remembers that his first attempt at fixing the lock was not to his customer's satisfaction, it was a sloppy job, and he further irritated his customer by returning to his truck to get additional parts to redo the job. The customer then paid him in cash, and, due to his fatigue, Jay forgot to give him change and a receipt. In short, Jay had committed every error that could put him in the camp of the typical one-star New York locksmith. As he predicted, the client posted a one-star review, but rather than leave the negative review standing, Jay used the slam on his reputation as a way of getting his foot back in the door.

Jay contacted the customer and apologized for the bad work and the missing change and receipt. He offered to give the customer a 50 percent discount on any future job. I wondered if Jay had asked the customer to take down his negative review, but he was adamant that just doing right by his client was enough. Jay makes the point that if you care enough about your work and show the customer your passion for doing things right, things will take care of themselves. The customer called a few days later with a small job, which, with a full night's rest, Jay completed to the customer's satisfaction, and the negative review was removed.

I asked Jay for his advice to new businesses. His first suggestion was to immediately claim your business on review sites. Stated another way, think of your business's Yelp page or Google reviews page as an extension of your own Web site. Take this opportunity to be as transparent as possible. If you look at Jay's page on Yelp you'll find that he put up as many details as possible. Include your contact information, pricing, and information about who you are and what makes your business special. Jay even produced a video that can be played from his page (this does require that you buy advertising from Yelp). In addition to Jay's advice, take a note from how he capitalized on a simple gap in the marketplace—the demand for honest, prompt, and courteous locksmiths in New York City. By reviewing reviews in your industry, do you find a common complaint, a recurring issue?

Jay's business has now expanded to two trucks, and he is in discussion to franchise his business nationwide. There is even talk of a reality television series based on his business. It all began with online consumer reviews.

By being genuine to your passion and transparent to the marketplace, you've taken the first two steps toward improving your business. The third step is based on a recurring theme that I picked up when talking to both business owners with top reviews as well as reviewers about their criteria for awarding five stars to a business. Both sides provided one simple suggestion: do something unexpected.

Rule 3: Make Reviews Central to the Conversation

Businesses that have successfully leveraged reviews have one commonality: that reviews aren't the sole focus of the business, but rather just a part of the conversation. For many years now, since the dawn of social media, businesses have had to alter the way they communicate with customers, moving from a broadcast model, or one-way conversation (print ads, radio, television), to a conversation where social-media sites facilitate two-way communication. In that vein, the discourse between businesses and customers on review forums is a central part of the conversation, but it's only a part.

Conversations continue to happen on Facebook, Twitter, and other social media sites. Mohawk Matt and Bolt Barbers is the perfect example of how reviews can become a central part of the conversation.

The Physical World

For bricks-and-mortar business owners, the conversation about your business can happen before your customer even walks through the door. When walking around town you're bound to see window stickers for TripAdvisor, Yelp, OpenTable, and others. Mohawk

Matt went the extra step to post some of his most notorious negative reviews in the shop window in his elaborate publicity stunt. More frequently, business owners are starting to display positive reviews that they've received in the same way that they might post a restaurant review from the local paper. Physical postings accomplish two things. First, they provide an advertising opportunity to let those unfamiliar with your business know that others have enjoyed the services and products at your establishment. Second, and more important, they show your current customers that you take customer opinions seriously, and that they matter to your business.

When I asked Jay the locksmith whether he ever asks his clients for reviews, his response was, "That's lame." Rather, he found ways to work reviews into the conversation, by asking new customers how they had heard about him. A simple window sticker or display of review quotes can have the same effect. When you follow my fifth rule, which we'll discuss in a few pages, the subtle clues posted outside your business send the message that if someone is happy with your service, she can repay the favor by posting a favorable review.

The Web

Many review sites provide feeds that allow you to post all of your reviews to your business's Web site. While it may seem to be counterintuitive to post all reviews to your site, there's good reason to do so.

As I mentioned in the first chapter, businesses that post product reviews on their pages found that conversions or purchases increased from 3 to 4.6 percent, depending on the number of reviews posted to the site. Even if you're not selling products on your page, posting reviews will help you keep your customers on your page, versus the inevitable result if you don't—many customers will leave your page to read another site's reviews, and then you risk losing your customer to a competitor.

In the late nineties it was common to be wary of posting reviews on a business Web site. I refer to this as "pre-Amazon" thinking. Competitors, marketers, and industry analysts, like those at Dataquest, predicted that Amazon's growing review database would ultimately hurt the business. In retrospect we know that reviews happen to be one of the key differentiators for Amazon. The massive amount of reviews turned Amazon into something more than just an online store; in addition to selling goods, Amazon's review ecosystem became an invaluable resource for its consumers.

While some reasoned that it was a risky move for Wyndham Hotels and Resorts to list all of their TripAdvisor ratings, the advantage of having reviews on the page quickly became obvious despite some of the properties having negative ratings. The chain's room booking increased after reviews were brought onto the reservations page, even for properties with overall negative reviews. Wyndham was able to keep its prospective guests on the reservations page, versus risking having those guests leave the page to go directly to TripAdvisor to consult ratings before making a travel decision and possibly choosing a competitor's hotel in the process.

There was another interesting by-product of having every property's reviews in such a critical part of the company's Web site; it provided a very transparent public display that increased accountability across the organization. After incorporating the review feed, from the executive team to the cleaning staff, employees began to meet to discuss issues pointed out in reviews. Reviews became more than a means to attract new guests to Wyndham; they became motivation for the entire staff to raise their game.

Social Media

The conversation doesn't end with a review and your response. Social media sites like Facebook, Twitter, and Instagram provide additional means to amplify your positive reviews (and in some cases, your negative reviews). Never one to shy away from controversy, Mohawk Matt extended his "People Hate Us on Yelp" campaign by also posting his negative Yelp reviews on Facebook. In an interesting twist, Matt asked Bolt Barbers' fans to reply to his negative reviews via Facebook comments to provide an interactive element for expanding the reach of his campaign. Negative PR stunt aside, businesses should consider taking a page from the Bolt Barbers playbook and post or tweet excerpts of positive reviews on social media as a way of expanding the reach of their online reviews.

Rule 4: Leverage Reviews for Insight and Motivation

Another commonality for businesses that have achieved success through reviews is the hyperattentiveness to online feedback.

Back at Hotel 41, much like the accountability that Wyndham's strategy has fostered, front-desk staff have become hyperaware of their online reviews, embracing them in the spirit of competition and measurement of guest satisfaction.

When a Hotel 41 guest writes a rare negative review, the staff immediately brings the review to management. In the case of a room that was reported to be too dimly lit, within a few hours of the review posting the hotel chain's managing director, hotel manager, and housekeeping staff all convened a meeting in the dimly lit room to assess how they could improve. A simple lightbulb change illustrates that in the race for the number-one spot, there are no trivial issues.

Before the online review era, satisfaction surveys and personal interactions were the only modes of feedback for business owners. All of that changed with the free access that businesses have to their own reviews, and the reviews of their competitors. Successful businesses in the review space are now engaged with online opinion at the owner (or management) level, and they encourage all of their employees to read, study, and learn from their reviews and those of their competitors. When employees actively engage with customers and work hard to make sure everyone has a five-star experience, they also become acutely aware of customers who are having negative experiences. If those same employees are motivated by online reviews, through intervening and doing their best to correct problems, they can prevent a negative posting.

Rule 5: Give Them Something to Write About

In addition to being transparent, the other element Jay mentions as responsible for his online review success is that he does something unexpected (that is, beyond showing up on time and well groomed). When he's finished with a job, and has taken extra time to make sure that he cleans his work area well, he'll also service the door he was working on by oiling the hinges. As Jay discovered by oiling door hinges, or Mohawk Matt with a twenty-two-foot shuffleboard table and PBR and root beer on tap, there are plenty of ways to be memorable. Providing a little something unexpected can go a long way to making your business memorable in your customers' eyes, like an amuse-bouche at a five-star restaurant.

In today's marketplace, as businesses compete on price, one of the disheartening side effects of review sites is that there can be a trend to commoditize products and services. Based on all the information available to consumers, they can reduce most decisions down to their lowest common denominator. One of the most effective antidotes to commoditization is to provide something that falls outside the equation, something unexpected and memorable.

As you read through the reviews of your highly rated competitors, focus on the five-star reviews. Look for a theme. Is there something extra that they're doing to garner five-star reviews that you're not? If you don't find anything in competitors' reviews, what about your own experiences? What have been the most memorable dinners, vacations, customer-support experiences? Ask yourself why they were memorable, and if there was something about those experiences that you could replicate in your business. Maybe it was something small, fulfilling a request, anticipating your need. Remember that feeling, and that it probably made you want to do something nice in return.

More than ten years ago I attended an informal birthday dinner with friends at our local Indian restaurant. Unbeknownst to us, the owner of this very small eatery overheard us talking about the fact that we were out celebrating one of our friends' birthday. The restaurant didn't have any desserts on hand, so the owner snuck out and purchased a birthday cake and candle from the grocery store down the street. A positive review and a decade later, I still tell that story, a testament to how memorable an unexpected and gracious act can be. If you're in a service industry, that act can be something like remembering a customer's name and their preferences. If you have an e-commerce business, making that connection might be as simple as putting a little free promotional item in packages to your customers.

These five rules to better reviews aren't just to increase the number of five-star ratings you'll receive (although if you do commit to these rules, you should see your ratings go up). By following these basic steps you will improve your reviews and reconnect with the passion that you have for what you do. You'll become a better business owner by communicating your value through transparency, and in giving your customers something to write about, you'll find new ways to build meaningful connections with them.

To review a business that has put these five rules into action, I decided to sit down for a cup of coffee with my new friend, café owner and partner Ramesh Manian. By all logical accounts, his

Station Café shouldn't have been successful. The coffee and sandwich shop by day, and Italian trattoria by night, was on the wrong side of the tracks in an industrial area of San Carlos, California. Though he had no professional hospitality experience prior to opening the Station Café, Ramesh did have two things going for him: having been the CEO of several Silicon Valley start-ups, he is a very astute businessman with a love of data, and he had an absolute passion for running an Italian café.

At ten A.M. during the week, the café still has a steady morning coffee flow of traffic. When I entered the door, I noticed Ramesh hugging two customers in line for coffee. Wearing a polo shirt and jeans and hair pulled back into a ponytail, Ramesh looked more like a New Age guru than an owner of an Italian café. He ushered me into a conference room off to the side of the main dining room filled with metal filing cabinets, a large wooden table, and office chairs that felt as though they were the last vestiges of a former use for this building.

Before heading over to visit the Station Café I checked out its Yelp page. I was surprised to see that such a small restaurant had four and a half stars with 120 reviews. They were awarded an OpenTable Diners' Choice Award in 2012, with four and a half stars and 13 reviews, and 5 reviews averaging four stars from TripAdvisor. It was clear that Ramesh was on top of his reviews, as he could recall most of the reviews, positive and negative. I asked him how his restaurant was doing, and he offered to show me his Yelp chart, turning his laptop around.

When I asked Ramesh what role reviews played in the launching of his restaurant café, he responded by saying, "I never did anything like this before. I started to understand how important it was to look at user reviews, and at the same time maybe not so important." When I told him I wasn't sure what he meant, he continued, "At the end of the day, no matter what you do, you need great food, great service, everything will work out." We talked about having a vision and being genuine to delivering on that vision.

As Ramesh left the room to answer a phone call, I thought about all the business owners I've spoken with while writing this book. I can clearly see two common themes that run through all my interviews, from Jay the locksmith and Mohawk Matt to all the others.

The first is passion. Each individual I've encountered who has realized success from online reviews started that journey with an absolute passion for what he does. According to Jonathan Raggett at Hotel 41, he made it very clear that in order for his hotel to operate at the level it does today, it requires the utmost passion for hospitality. "Hospitality is one of the first things I look for when I'm hiring at the hotel. Everyone must have a passion for hospitality."

The second common theme is staying genuine to your goals. As we begin the exercise of assessing your business based on user reviews, it's very important to start with a clear vision of who you are and how you plan to run your business. When Ramesh says that reviews aren't always so important, he is referring to the reviews of those who do not share the same goals. If you blindly follow what reviews are telling you to do without considering how those points expressed online mesh with your vision, you are in danger of going off the rails.

We'll revisit the five rules that form your business strategy for leveraging online reviews, but more important, this exercise will help you take the first steps in solidifying your overall business mission, and your support and marketing strategies. Who are you? What are you? These are the very basic questions that you should be able to answer quickly. Known in the start-up world as your elevator pitch, you should be able to explain to someone in a ten- to thirty-second elevator ride what it is that your business delivers. Once you have your elevator pitch figured out, the first question you'll need to ask yourself is, how am I unique? What do I do that's different from what exists in the marketplace? If you can't answer that question, you need to rethink your pitch, or resign yourself to the fact that you are a commodity business that will have to survive on thin margins as you compete with a number of other businesses that can't distinguish themselves.

Jay the locksmith wanted to differentiate himself from the crowded field of New York City locksmiths in a very simple way. His vision was to set himself apart by being prompt and courteous. He also wanted to be as transparent as possible regarding what he charges to come out and fix your lock. Compare that to Mohawk Matt, who had a grandiose vision of creating a barbershop that provided an unparalleled, and sometime irreverent, experience, complete with big-screen TVs, shuffleboard table (which is now level), and root beer and PBR on draft.

Before we move on, this is the point where you need to pause and ask yourself, how passionate am I for this business that I've described? Am I passionate enough that those who frequent my business will be moved to go online and write a review? Once you have your vision in focus, the next step will be to break down that vision into all the elements of products and service. Of course this step will vary by what line of business you're in. Imagine you own a midrange boutique hotel. If your hotel vision is to provide your guests with a hassle-free, welcoming environment that is built around providing all the comforts of home, you might break that vision down to the following elements:

- Reservation

- Check-in

- Hotel amenities

- Room amenities

- Housekeeping

- Room service

Now flesh out each element of service. How will you deliver that service in line with your vision, and, if appropriate, how will you differentiate yourself from the competition? Since you're a smaller boutique hotel, you decide not to outsource your reservations during business hours, and have the reservation phone number ring to the hotel's front desk. Perhaps you would like your staff trained in using specific terms, to ask specific questions during the reservation process so that you can deliver on your vision of a welcoming environment.

Taking a page from Jay the locksmith's playbook, once you have finished fleshing out all the elements of your vision, the second step is to make your vision transparent. Now that you've decided what you believe to be the perfect experience, let your customers and potential customers know by publishing the important points of your vision.

The concept of being transparent serves several purposes; first, it's a form of marketing to let your potential customers know exactly what it is that you intend to deliver, but in terms of reviews, the important thing is that you are setting expectations for your potential reviewers. Today we have so many channels through which we can communicate with our customers and prospects. We can post information to our Web site and to a Facebook page, pictures on Instagram, terse statements via Twitter, but, most important, most review sites give the business owner the ability to post text, images, and videos to their review page. If you deliver on what you promised, you stand a far greater chance of garnering positive reviews. What you will hopefully mitigate is unmet or unreasonable expectations.

Following our example, if you decide not to outsource your reservations, you could make a statement on your Web site, Facebook page, and review pages that reads:

> We value your business and want to personally make sure
> we can answer all your questions regarding our hotel and
> its surroundings, that's why we won't send your call off
> to a call center in another part of the country or world . . .

What can you do (without too great of an impact on revenue) to make your business memorable in the minds of your customers?

Recently I stayed at a Starwood property where I have status with their affinity program. One perk of the Starwood program is that you get a choice of amenities at check-in (a free movie, a beer and popcorn, free parking, extra affinity points, etc.). Delivering on the vision of providing a welcoming environment, what if you were to offer amenities to your guests during the reservation process as a way of setting the tone for the stay and giving them something to look forward to?

> Thank you for your reservation, Mr. Smith. Before I let you go we want to make sure you have a relaxing stay with us. We have a number of amenities for you to choose from. . . .

Sometimes it's a great idea to leave a lasting impression at the end of an experience. At a recent hotel stay, everything about the service was top-notch and I had no complaints. As we checked out of the hotel we were escorted to our car by the bellman, who was wheeling our luggage. He loaded the luggage into the trunk of our car, and another bellman offered us some cold water for the road, a nice touch that we've experienced at other hotels and resorts. Then I noticed, propped up on the console of the car dashboard, a cellophane bag of candy with a thank-you note from the hotel staff. That little bag of candy probably cost no more than fifty cents to the hotel, but the impression of an unexpected little gift at the end of a stay (as opposed to a fruit basket at the beginning) was both appreciated and memorable.

In chapter 7 we will discuss word-of-mouth marketing and what drives consumers to generate and share experiences. When you provide a positive but also highly memorable experience, you have increased the likelihood of securing another five-star review.

Assessment

Keep your vision and breakdown steps handy as we take the next step of leveraging online reviews by revisiting your business's reviews. When I sat down with Ramesh, he had a very good recommendation. Throw out the first ten reviews you ever received, as they might give you a false sense of security. Ramesh knows that during the first days of your business you're likely to have friends and family visit; their bias toward good reviews, as well as those from customers who just want to help out by publicizing the fact that you're new, can lead to a positive skew in your ratings. If you have enough reviews to spare for the analysis, then toss out these first ten; if not, then consider any potential skews as you analyze your data.

Keep a piece of scratch paper nearby or a blank Word document open to record your first impressions of the last year's reviews for your business. As you go through the reviews on the first pass, your objective is to read through them to determine if there are any recurring themes. Did diners point out that they had to wait a long time for service? Did they complain about the food or the cleanliness of the restrooms? Were there positive trends? Were any dishes praised in multiple reviews? How about servers, and decor? Now take out your vision and break it down. Did the reviews that you read for the last year cover the items that you listed in your breakdown? Were there any items reviewed that didn't make it into your breakdown list?

Now is the time to reassess your vision and elements list. Perhaps there are some criticisms in your reviews that would have you alter your vision to satisfy. You have to decide if your vision is complete or if you should adapt based on overall criticism.

As we take the next pass, create two columns next to the elements of your vision, labeling one column "positive" and one "negative." As you read through your reviews, note positive and negative comments that are associated with every element of your vision.

Now that you've completed the second pass, take a step back. Did you learn anything from this exercise? Was there something that your customers responded to positively that was a surprise to you? In looking at the negative comments, did the analysis highlight problems that you were already aware of? Were there any surprises?

To find an application of this exercise I didn't have to go far, just a few miles down the road to a local café. Caffe Roma is a family business comprising three Italian coffee shops in the San Francisco Bay Area. Right off the 101, Irene's patrons range from the retired set to young telecommuters, as well as travelers on their way from or to San Francisco International Airport only a few miles up the road. With such an eclectic mix of customers, online reviews are an important source of new business.

While Caffe Roma's reviews were mostly positive, after doing the second pass I noticed some recurring themes. When someone would order a pastry and ask that it be heated, the staff often forgot about the item and left it in the oven too long, so that it dried out and burned. This was a problem that could be remedied with staff training. A more challenging issue arose out of the internal analysis. When Irene is at the café, she has an uncanny ability to remember everyone's name, even after meeting someone only once. Her memory, along with her skills in hospitality, make her customers feel like they're part of the family. In reviewing reviews of her restaurant, some of the complaints about management and service made it clear that when Irene is not at the café, the atmosphere changes. This leads to an action item of finding a way to impart the feeling of family when Irene can't be at the café.

There are countless things that can be learned by studying the reviews of your own business. By backing up and reading reviews with a critical eye, we can find areas for improvement that were not very apparent. To gain even greater insight, we can expand our focus to analyzing competitors' review traffic.

I spent another morning with Ramesh discussing how, as a high-tech executive turned chef, he's leveraged online review data to improve his café/restaurant. One of the challenges that he faced with his new venture was that it is "a little schizophrenic. It's a coffee bar and a restaurant; sometimes it's hard to explain that on Yelp or OpenTable." Ramesh also shared some of the challenges he's had with OpenTable reviewers versus consumer critics on Yelp. "It's not that OpenTable reviewers are more critical, it's that they are expecting a different type of experience than the Yelper," he explains. "Yelp reviewers are looking for the best coffee or the best food at a good price. OpenTable reviewers are different; it's more about the dining experience."

On OpenTable, along with supplying a narrative review, reviewers are asked to rate a restaurant for its food, ambience, service, and noise level. Given Station Café's location in an industrial section of town, and the sparse decorating in the dining area, it wasn't a surprise to Ramesh that he was receiving low scores for ambience. Ramesh considered what he could do to raise his score, so he painted the walls of the restaurant a subtle Restoration Hardware green, and added some framed pictures to the walls. His score went up immediately. "Sometimes it's the small things that make a difference," Ramesh confides.

A few months after I met with Ramesh, he e-mailed me to let me know that he was closing the Station Café. He decided that he needed to relocate the restaurant to a better area. He's since gone back to the tech world, but he's looking for a new spot to reopen the business. "It may take three months, or maybe a year," but he's waiting till he finds just the right location. With 157 reviews and an average rating of four and a half stars on Yelp, Ramesh's choice to leave the restaurant business doesn't undermine his insights into how the industry works. It does underscore just how competitive and difficult it is to run a small business—even when you have reviews on your side.

7.

Dealing with Reviews:
After the Fact

★ ★ ★ ★ ★

Now that you understand your reviews, and your competitors'
reviews, you'll need to know how to jump in and participate in
the online review channel. Much like marketing in social media
(Facebook, Twitter, YouTube), the online review channel is con-
versational, not a one-sided broadcast. There are some basic
rules you should follow when participating in online review forums, but before we get there let's look at a nontraditional approach to dealing with reviews after the fact.

While most people use bad reviews as a reason to avoid online
review sites, Mohawk Matt provided us with a perfect example
of harnessing the power of negative reviews. Matt realized a
counterintuitive fact that people love to talk about negative reviews, and now other businesses have replicated the use of negative reviews for publicity. In the Little Italy district of San Diego,
Arsalun Tafazoli, co-owner of gastropub Craft and Commerce,
decided to vent his frustration in an unusual way. If you visit the
restaurant's restroom, you'll be treated to a reading of Craft and

Commerce's one-star reviews played over speakers in the bathroom. Reviews include this clip from A.I.:

> I have never been in a place that tries so hard. This place is the epicenter of those assholes with the mustaches. . . . Next, the place is jammed with hipsters eating corn dogs . . .

Or this clip from A.L.:

> The food doesn't live up to the hype. Biscuits that taste like the ones from Red Lobster but half the size. Average fried chicken. We've had better mussels at Bleu Boheme. And the bacon ice cream sandwich? Re: bacon—just because it's trendy, doesn't mean you have to do it.[1]

Despite their anti-Yelp positions, both business owners received considerable press coverage from their publicity stunts. As we'll see later, in some cases, irreverent campaigns that make fun of all the controversy surrounding online reviews can be very successful, and ironically there is a good chance that the review community will embrace them as well.

Beyond publicity stunts, getting consumers to spread the word about their experiences isn't a new concept. Many credit psychologist George Silverman with coining the phrase *word-of-mouth marketing*, or WOM. When Silverman conducted focus groups on physicians in the 1970s, he noticed that one or two physicians who had a good experience with a drug could sway an entire room of skeptics. "This minority could even change the minds of doctors who had prescribed the drug in the past and had a negative experience."[2]

According to research on how word of mouth spreads, individuals are much more likely to generate positive reviews about experiences that they have and are more likely to pass along, or tell friends about, negative reviews that they have read.[3] The reasoning behind the drive to write positive reviews but spread negative reviews goes to the primary question of why we talk about products at all. Earlier theories around WOM marketing have included a list of why individuals might spread a positive message, including a desire to help a company, altruism, product involvement, desire to demonstrate expertise, and resolution of cognitive dissonance, to name a few.[4] In their research on why people write reviews, professors Matteo De Angelis of the University of Wisconsin and Andrea Bonezzi of NYU School of Business assert that it is because we simply want to feel better about ourselves. By talking about our positive experiences we reinforce that we make smart decisions.

Yet the story can't be that simple, or else everyone would choose between writing five-star reviews or staying quiet. According to Yelp, 13 percent of all reviews have one star, two stars make up 8 percent, while four- and five-star reviews are 27 percent and 39 percent, respectively.[5] So why do some consumers pen the 13 percent of one-star reviews? According to Bonezzi's research, when something bad happens to you, when someone doesn't treat you well, you feel the need to compensate. Prior to online review sites, you might have compensated by telling your friends and family what a horrible experience you had with the offending business. Today, if a business has made you really angry, you can harm it by taking your opinions online.

There's also the interesting insight that consumers are most likely to spread negative commentary about someone else's experience. In the world of online reviews, this might translate to someone telling their friends or family about a negative review that they read on TripAdvisor or Yelp. We spread negative information about businesses for the same reason that we trill about the new restaurant we just discovered: we want to feel better about ourselves. By sharing stories of how somebody experienced a poor meal, was ripped off by a small business, or had a horrible customer service issue, we feel a little more confident that we were smart enough to avoid such a negative experience.

The difference between the spread of positive and negative word of mouth accounts for the genius behind Mohawk Matt's "People Hate Us on Yelp" campaign. In a review that he reprinted in his self-published book, *People Hate Us on Yelp—Excerpts from Bolt Barbers Worst Reviews,* Matt includes the three-star review from I.B., who had a bloody experience:

> The hairdresser managed to cut the moles on my neck—making me bleed. It wasn't too bad, but she successfully cut two of two I got there. I don't like it when barbers make me bleed.

Most shop owners would shudder at the thought of blasting out that one of the staff barbers accidentally cut a customer. Matt, however, not only reprinted and freely shared this unfortunate customer experience but also responded online and in the book by admitting the incident.

> [Our barber] greatly regrets the accidental surgical mole removal which did occur at Bolt Barbers. We like to leave the neckline on our dudes clean-shaven. But this hairy beast had a thick plush of hair covering his neck and upper back.

By sharing and publicizing his negative reviews in laminated pages in the barbershop's waiting area, posting them on the window of busy Spring Street in downtown Los Angeles, and pasting them into his fan page on Facebook for his clients to see (and spread via likes and comments), Matt has harnessed the power of negative word of mouth.

Mohawk Matt's innovative negative viral marketing campaign would work for any business that might thrive from a more irreverent approach to customer service. I doubt that the Four Seasons hotel chain or Thomas Keller's French Laundry would be able to pull off this type of snarky campaign. That being said, Matt's innovative response to online customer opinions does demonstrate some important takeaways.

Don't Let a Little Negative Feedback Scare You Away from Reading Reviews

As I've mentioned, negative reviews feel more than just unfair. They publicly insult our life's work, our dreams, and often from an anonymous account. Matt, however, with the power of conviction behind his vision of creating Bolt Barbers, was able to embrace his negative reviews, both as a vehicle for his viral "People Hate Us on Yelp" campaign as well as for traditional ways to improve his shop's customer service. When you know who you are and what you're trying to accomplish, reading your negative reviews becomes a more palatable experience.

One of the most common questions business owners have is whether to respond to online reviews of their business. Lecturer David Evans, along with graduate students at the University of Washington, set out to study that specific question. They exposed 259 readers to randomly selected mock-ups of a Yelp business profile and measured the readers' reactions. The mock-up profiles shown to the subjects included a profile only; a profile with a negative review and no response from the owner; a profile, a negative review, and a combative response; a profile with a negative review and a constructive response; and, finally, a profile, a negative review, and a constructive response that included PR best practices. When asked how likely they would be to go to the restaurant for the mock-up profiles that they had seen on a scale of 1 (not likely), 2 (somewhat likely), or 3 (likely), the profile with no negative reviews ranked highest, at 1.89, while the lowest score went to the profile where there was a negative review and no response (1.24).[6]

According to this research, even a combative response from the owner was better than no response at all. The takeaway from this study is that you should always respond to negative reviews of your business.

While there is limited research to answer whether you should reply to positive reviews, research would seem to indicate that it's always best to respond. In the case of a positive review, a simple thank-you will suffice, or you can learn from Jonathan Raggett's technique of using the response to the positive review as an opportunity to reinforce some of the positive messages that go along with your vision.

If you comment on a positive review, remember to be unique in each response—no one wants to feel that they've been pandered to.

What About Positive Reviews?

While it's clear that there is a benefit to responding to negative reviews, should we give positive reviews the same consideration?

It's unlikely that a management response to a positive review will motivate a reader to purchase, but there are some positive benefits from giving attention to your four- and five-star reviews. Based on interviews with Elite Yelpers and Top Contributors from TripAdvisor, the consensus is that top reviewers appreciate a thank-you from management for both positive and negative reviews.

From a branding perspective, just as we discussed with negative reviews, owner/manager comments are an opportunity for you to reinforce a particular part of your brand or a highlight of the user's experience. Jonathan Raggett, the managing director at Hotel 41's parent company, Red Carnation Hotels, is a master at leveraging the positive review.

Jonathan described a positive review that the hotel's restaurant,

Bbar, received from a guest. Having stopped by the table during the guest's dinner, Jonathan engaged the guest in conversation and learned that the guest loved his main course so much that he declared it one of the best fish dishes he had ever had. In a corresponding positive review on TripAdvisor, Jonathan took the opportunity to thank the guest while at the same time mentioning how happy he was that the guest enjoyed what he called "the best fish dish that he had ever had."

Perhaps it's an inborn trait that executives at the top of their game have in the hospitality industry, but in his response, Jonathan knew that if a customer has a positive experience with what should be a pleasure-based activity (like eating), then you don't go down the path of explaining the specifics of why the guest enjoyed meal, but rather you just reinforce the emotion. As with negative reviews, the one thing that you want to avoid in replying to positive reviews is the use of boilerplate language. You should respond to positive reviews only when you can add something unique and emotionally reinforcing to the post.

The policy at the Four Seasons in Austin is to respond to 100 percent of all their negative reviews on TripAdvisor and Yelp, and 80 percent of their positive reviews. According to the staff at Four Seasons corporate, responding to online reviews is one aspect of their social media program. I had a chance to sit down with Andrew Gillespie, the assistant director for reservation operations at Four Seasons corporate, and he shared the challenge and opportunities presented in conversing with their guests via online social channels.

Best Practices for Replying to Negative Reviews

Rule 1: Start with a Simple Thank-You

It sounds counterintuitive, but reviewers appreciate knowing that a manager or owner of a business has taken the time to read their complaint and respond specifically to the issues they had problems with. While the length of the reviewers' negative posts may vary from a single-sentence review to a thousand-word diatribe on the harms suffered at your establishment, the thank-you serves two purposes: first, it acknowledges that the owner or manager appreciates the feedback; and second, the owner or manager demonstrates that he is taking the high road and won't be dragged into a yelling match in the most public of forums. The next rule is the most important, and unfortunately the most violated of all the rules.

Rule 2: Tailor Your Response So That It Is Unique, Sincere, and Directly Addresses the Complaint

Whether your disappointed customer is a communitarian, a citizen critic, a one-star assassin, or even a fraud, your response should be tailored to the specific complaint. While it wasn't addressed in the University of Washington study, from my qualitative interviews with high-volume reviewers on Yelp and TripAdvisor, nothing aggravates a reviewer (and the millions of potential customers reading your response) more than getting the same boilerplate response. Reference back to the specifics that your reviewer provided in their review so that everyone understands your commitment to providing superior service.

Rule 3: Now Is the Time to Explain the Cupcake

Writing your response with the goal of providing specific information as to why something went wrong with a customer's experience is an easy way to tailor your response, but also a great way to diffuse a difficult situation.

Rule 4: Frame Your Response with Your End Point

Finish your response by reiterating your vision for your business, and describe how the reviewer's experience departed from how you envision your company. This is your opportunity to respond to a negative complaint by reinforcing a positive brand message for you and your company. If, for example, you run a general contracting business and your vision for your company is to provide superior construction for your clients based on honesty, excellent communications, and commitment to craftsmanship, you might respond to a one-star review that claimed you had overbilled a client with the following end-point framing:

> Dear Mr. Smith, I was disappointed to hear that you had issues with the final billing for our construction project on your home. When I started this business ten years ago, I had a vision of setting myself apart from the competition by providing superior craftsmanship while providing my clients with excellent communications regarding project

timing so that there would be no surprises. From reading your review it appears that we had a communication breakdown that led to this misunderstanding. As my business is built on trust, I will be looking into how this matter could have been handled differently.

Rule 5: Offer to Connect Directly

End your response to each negative review by offering to discuss the matter further and providing the reviewer with your contact information. If you prefer to keep your contact information private, state in your response that you will be sending the reviewer a direct message with your contact information so that you can discuss the matter further.

Most experts agree that you should refrain from publicly offering any compensation to a reviewer for a negative experience, even if it is customary in your business to offer such compensation. Since online review sites are open forums that can be read by anyone, unscrupulous future reviewers might try to extract similar benefits based on fraudulent claims. If you are still compelled to offer a reviewer a comp, do so via direct or private message.

8

★ ★ ★ ★ ★

Dealing with Reviews Preemptively

★ ★ ★ ★ ★

Rather than waiting by your laptop screen or nervously hitting the refresh button on your smartphone for those first reviews, there are some things that you can do to increase the chances that your reviews will be positive.

At the time of this writing, Jay's 171 reviews were almost exclusively five stars. Jay's opinion that asking clients for reviews is "lame" is in keeping with how Yelp feels on the topic. Darnell Holloway at Yelp warns that if you aggressively pursue your customers for reviews, you might trigger reviews that will be filtered, and you might alienate customers by making them feel like promotional vehicles for better ratings. Not all review sites feel the same way as Yelp. The TripAdvisor for Business service offers TripConnect, a software package that, among other features, provides an e-mail engine to automatically e-mail a hotel's guests after checkout to request an online review at TripAdvisor. Likewise, several online retailers solicit reviews for their sites' review systems (having recognized that increased reviews equate to increased sales). You shouldn't take TripAdvisor's actions as license to go after reviews yourself. Holloway does have a point that your customers might feel used, and their memory of your excellent product or service might be marred by feeling used through an online review request. Many retailers are still figuring out the best way to ask for a review, and some got it completely wrong.

Up until the release of iOS 4 in 2010, the Apple iTunes store had what I believe to be an infamous review collection system that was hated by most application developers. The feature, which was called "review on delete," did exactly as the name implies; when you deleted an application from your device, a dialogue box appeared on your screen asking you to rate the application. Apple, which has some of the most sophisticated marketing minds in the industry, was generating a lot of reviews for the App Store, but those reviews were skewing toward the negative. When you ask for a review only when someone is in the process of deleting an app, you have a selection bias toward consumers who have grown tired of the application or who never liked it in the first place.

If you're not going to ask, then how do you prompt your customers to write a positive review? Jay has some suggestions. While he won't ask his customers to review his business, he will find ways of discussing the topic of online reviews. For example, if he's called out on a job to help a tourist get back into an Airbnb apartment that they're locked out of, he'll first ask how they found him (tourists often use Yelp to find services like locksmiths, as they're unfamiliar with the neighborhood). He'll then remark that he gets a lot of business from Yelp. Next, as he does with all his customers, he goes out of his way to suggest some restaurants or things to see in the city. By simply identifying that reviews are important to his business and then going out of his way to be nice to his clients, they want to do something nice in return. If Jay is called out on a job for a local, he'll do the same thing. When making small talk, Jay will ask what the customer's favorite restaurant or bar is, he'll share some of his recommendations, and, as with the tourist, he'll build rapport with the customer so that they will want to review Lockbusters after the job is complete.

There are many ways to set the stage for positive reviews. I think back to the Red Carnation hotel chain and the 41. Though I was never asked to review the hotel, I was aware of how important the site was to their business. Relaxing in the library of the Hotel 41, I notice the room has a cozy feel, with glass atrium ceilings and the soft patter of a typical London rain, while two lit fireplaces provide warmth against the weather. The floorboards creek as the staff walks by, hinting to the age of the place. The 41's library is the social hub of the small boutique hotel. As with most hotels in London, the 41's standard rooms are small, but since I spend the majority of my time in the library, I hardly notice. While here, I have the opportunity to observe how the staff has kept its number-one rating of all London hotels uninterrupted for so many years. Andrew, the hotel's resident manager, is the first to stop by, and makes the rounds several times each morning to engage the guests in conversation. "I trust you're having a wonderful stay?" "What are your plans for the weekend?" "Can we help make any arrangements for you?" Unlike at other hotels where you would make your way to the concierge desk to inquire about activities, the staff at 41 is trained to go to the guests and anticipate their needs. This is all done in a very subtle way so that the guests don't feel like the staff is overstepping their bounds. The interaction with the staff feels like a conversation with friends and family. From the moment I step into the narrow downstairs lobby off Victoria Street to leaving a sincere positive review on TripAdvisor, it all feels like part of the conversation.

Taking a cue from the 41, the goal for your business is to increase your chances of getting positive reviews. One of the best ways to do that is to enter the review process during the experience, not after the fact, when you feel the compulsion to argue a negative review in an open forum.

When you analyze a consumer review, you should view it not as a single statement issued by one of your customers but instead as part of a larger conversation that started when the customer first interacted with your business all the way through to your thank-you for leaving a positive review. How you and your staff interact with customers and the nature of what type of products or services your business provides can make the difference in getting your customers engaged to write positive reviews.

The advent of online consumer reviews has also provided a new dimension to word-of-mouth marketing. While "trusted source" becomes more tenuous, the amplification of an opinion about a restaurant's ambience, the quality of a haircut, or the cleanliness of a hotel room takes those personal face-to-face recommendations and makes them both public and easily discoverable. To the extent that those recommendations come from your social network "friend," the recommendations also become trusted.

Explaining the Cupcake

Professor Sarah Moore at the University of Alberta conducted research on the psychology of the review writer and what the effect of writing reviews has on the overall perception about an experience. While there is extensive research on how word of mouth spreads, there's been little research on how word of mouth affects the person spreading the information. Moore's research found that, based on the type of experience, reinforcing certain messages had the potential to amplify some feelings or dampen others.

To test her theory Moore conducted several experiments. In the first experiment she analyzed the text of Amazon book reviews (fiction) for explaining language (words used to describe why the consumer liked the book, such as "I bought this splendid book because it was a best seller") and for nonexplaining language ("I bought this book online"). She found that books with extreme ratings (one or five stars) had less explaining language, and that those that had moderate ratings (three stars) had more explaining language.

In the second part of the test, 102 students had to describe a pleasurable experience (going to a movie, going on vacation, dining out), and then explain in a written essay why the experience was pleasurable. Moore found that subjects who were able to describe why their experience was pleasurable were less likely to spread the word about the experience using WOM.

In the final portion, users were asked to fill in the blanks of online reviews similar to Amazon or Yelp reviews for both hedonic, or pleasurable, experiences and for utilitarian experiences.

Some in the group were given forms forcing them to use explaining language, while others received forms that focused on nonexplaining language. After completing the forms, the students were asked to rate their pleasurable or utilitarian experience, as well as their likelihood to tell others about it. Those subjects who explained a pleasurable experience ranked their experience as moderate, while those who were not prompted for explaining language rated their positive experience as more pleasurable. The utilitarian group found the opposite to be true. Explaining language increased the rating of positive products and decreased the rating for negative products, while nonexplaining language led to moderate reviews.

According to Moore, one of the obvious goals of word-of-mouth marketing is that the consumer tells not one but many people. If we look at what we say and how we say it, we should first address how our conversations with customers increase the chances of positive WOM while decreasing the chances of negative WOM. Moore's suggestion to businesses regarding their reviews is to first consider the type of product or service available; is it a hedonic product or service (a hotel room, a meal, a movie, music) or is it utilitarian (an airline flight, a USB drive, a doctor's visit)? If you are selling a pleasurable product or service and your customer enjoyed their experience, you shouldn't use explaining language when conversing with them. So if you're visiting tables in a restaurant and a diner says they love their meal, don't explain the recipe; rather, say that you're glad they're having such a wonderful experience. If, however, your guest is having a horrible meal, it's time to explain what might have gone wrong (which should serve to mitigate the negative feelings). Business owners should do the opposite with utilitarian services.

Seeding word of mouth isn't a simple process. Maintaining the level of enthusiasm that would cause a reviewer to share their experience with multiple people through review sites requires an understanding of the reviewer's experience and the type of emotion they associate with their experience. Many business owners might think that managing reviews means responding on review Web sites to remedy a bad experience or thank someone for a positive review, but Moore's research indicates that the conversation should probably begin much earlier, during the actual delivery of service.

According to Moore, given the dichotomy between hedonic and utilitarian encounters, someone who provides a primarily utilitarian experience, like Jay the locksmith, should use a different communication strategy than someone like Mohawk Matt, whose customers' experiences might lean more toward the hedonic.

Moore's research[1] shows that how a reviewer writes about a specific experience will have a polarizing effect or will mediate their emotions, and that effect depends on which type of experience it is and how the reviewer writes about it. Essentially, both the conversation you have with your customers about their experience as well as the act of writing a review can change your customer's view of that experience.

Imagine the most amazing cupcake you've ever had. If you were asked why you loved that cupcake so much, Moore's research would indicate that your explanation would mediate the experience; for example, you might reason that you loved the cupcake because the center had a rich chocolate filling. This exercise of explaining what you specifically liked causes you to rationalize all the reasons you had for enjoying the cupcake as much as you did. In this process, you begin to remove the emotions from the equation, or the whole reason that you fell in love with that cupcake in the beginning.

What business owners say to their customers can alter the likelihood of reviews and the ratings customers will give them. How might these insights help business owners generate more positive reviews in the real world? If you're a restaurant owner circulating in the dining room, Moore's findings suggest that you should approach each table and assess the diners' overall perception of their meals. If the patron is having a wonderful experience, you want to keep them in the moment and in the emotion by verbally reinforcing their positive feelings. For example, by saying "I'm thrilled that you're having such a wonderful meal," you stand a better chance of those positive emotions being transmitted into an online review. What you don't want to do in this scenario is explain to the diner why they enjoyed a dish so much. Listing ingredients or explaining the unique approach you have to making crème brûlée might cause the diner to write about those specific facts, and the diner's positive emotions about their dessert will likely dissipate as they rationalize their now utilitarian experience in a less euphoric user review. On the other hand, if you find that a diner is having a disappointing experience, explaining the recipe might be exactly what you need to do. With a negative experience you want to start the discussion with an apology. Next, you want to find a way to remedy that experience, by fixing the problem or providing some means of comping the guest. Most hospitality professionals will stop there, but you should want to go one step further. In discussing why the problem occurred, your goal is to mitigate all the negative emotions that your customer had with the experience by explaining exactly what caused the problem and validating their disappointment.

When it comes to emotional keywords you should focus on, when reinforcing a positive hedonic experience, you've already done most of the work. Return to the elements that you listed in your end-point exercise, and add an emotion to each of the elements that you identified. For the café example previously used, you wanted customers to feel connected with your business, so you took a personal interest, remembering their drink or their name. The emotional key that you would attach to this element is simply "connected." Whether it was a hedonic or a utilitarian experience, when you give the customer, and potential reviewer, a specific explanation as to why they've had a disappointing experience, it is likely that the diner's negative emotions will become less powerful, which should translate into a less negative review.

Jonathan Raggett, the managing director of Red Carnation Hotels (including Hotel 41), has found a way of starting the conversation during a customer's experience, then continuing that conversation online by responding publicly to a positive online review.

Jonathan recalls speaking with a guest about a dinner he was enjoying at the hotel's restaurant. When Jonathan asked the guest how he was enjoying his meal, the guest said that his main course was the best fish he had ever eaten. Jonathan's conversation began at the experience. When he checked on his diner, he focused on the diner's positive emotion by asking questions that would cause the diner to relive a very positive memory. When the diner went on to review his experience online, Jonathan thanked the guest publicly for posting such a positive review and used the opportunity to also thank the guest for telling him that his entrée was the best fish dish that he had ever had (a point that the guest failed to mention in his review). Rather than just commenting on a negative, Jonathan used the positive review as an opportunity to reinforce the guest's experience, continuing to keep to the emotion.

While reviews based on emotional or hedonic experiences can mediate or lessen their severity, utilitarian experiences provide the opportunity and challenge of polarizing reviewers to the extremes. If your business deals with a utilitarian product or service, by going into the details of a positive experience, you provide the reviewer with the ammunition to explain how a specific product or service fits their needs. Conversely, keeping away from the details of a negative experience will keep the reviewer from further solidifying it.

For example, if you sell USB thumb drives as your primary business, your chances of having a positive post increase if the reviewer specifically explains the reasons why he found the size, speed, or design of your drive to be superior to the rest. In Jay's case, having a lock fixed is a utilitarian experience. With a utilitarian service, if something goes wrong, the best way to respond is to explain in specific terms what happened, and how you would fix the problem in the future. When Jay the locksmith had that bad night and botched the job, he sought to mitigate the negative feelings that his customer might have had. By understanding your customer's frame of mind (happy or upset) and the nature of what they are consuming, you have identified the key variables to help guide the conversation.

Asking for the Review

Should you ever ask for the review? It's probably one of the most debated questions surrounding reviews. There are several review sites that actively seek out feedback from consumers. If you buy an app from the iTunes store, you'll be prompted to review your purchase. When you finish reading a book on your Kindle, Amazon will prompt you for a review. In 2013, TripAdvisor instituted a program to combine efforts with hotels to blast e-mails to all their clients' e-mail lists asking for more reviews.

It might seem like the efforts to build critical mass of reviews is giving business owners license to do the same, but this isn't the case. When I ask top-reviewed businesses whether they ask for the review, the response is an unequivocal no. Imagine you are ending a wonderful meal or you had a great customer service experience, and how your impression of that experience might change when the waiter or customer service personnel asks you to go online and review their business. It's as though the request to review cancels out the positive feelings you had about the experience, and now you're questioning the motives of the business. Do they truly value me as a customer, or do they see me as a vehicle to get their next five-star review?

If you're not going to ask for the review, how do you increase the chances of getting those good reviews? The answer is to let it happen organically, with a little push. When Jay interacts with his customer, he looks for the opportunity to chat, and will usually mention Yelp or Angie's List (depending on his client's age) and ask what some of his favorite Yelp finds are, like best restaurant bar. What Jay is doing intuitively is savvy. In bringing up a review site, he's associated himself with the site in the customer's mind, but, even more important, by having the client talk about some of his favorites, he's reinforcing his work with good feelings, and increasing the chances that if the client reviews him it will be positive.

Extending the Conversation

Today's consumer is multichanneled; she communicates through e-mail, text, Twitter, Facebook, Pinterest, Instagram, and the list goes on. To have a comprehensive consumer review strategy, you have to come to terms with the fact that reviews can happen across any of these channels. A customer having a bad experience at your business could decide to circumvent Yelp or Google reviews and go directly to tweeting their dissatisfaction, just as an amazing experience could end up as an Instagram photo or a Facebook post.

Part of a successful review strategy is to set up notifications across all of those surfaces so that you'll know when your brand is being discussed. In line with his brand of extreme marketing, when Bolt Barbers receives a one-star review, Mohawk Matt will add the review to his Facebook fan page and ask his Facebook fans how he should respond; he'll then take his favorite fan responses and add them to the owner response field on Yelp.

When extending your review conversation to other channels, keep all the five rules in mind, and be especially genuine and transparent. You should carry your vision through all communication platforms, from a Yelp or TripAdvisor review response to Twitter and Facebook posts. If a customer reaches out to you, it's your opportunity to get your message across and talk about what customers can expect from you. You should also circulate traffic as much as possible. Link Yelp reviews to your business's Facebook page, and link your Twitter account with your Facebook status updates. If a customer writes a good review and you have their Twitter handle, link to it by sending a thank-you via Twitter. Always focus on leveraging social media to increase your exposure.

9

★★★★★

Business Among "Friends"

* * * * *

In the online review era, when customer opinion can make such a big difference to your bottom line, many business owners realize they should treat their customers like friends and family. You might have noticed as a consumer that more business owners are crossing the business/friend barrier. It seems like the best approach to encouraging positive reviews and discouraging negative ones, as a friend ordinarily wouldn't purposefully try to hurt your business by posting a negative online review.

For the most part, this strategy works well, and no doubt many business owners are truly trying to be friendly, but those same business owners are discovering that there can be a backlash to the friend approach. Though friendliness is important, you are still in a business relationship; you're selling them products or services and they're paying you in return. What happens when a business objective requires you to treat your friend like a customer rather than a buddy? Business owners will attest that this scenario will likely lead to a very uncomfortable interaction, and an upset customer.

Back in Millbrae, California, I had a chance to sit down with Irene from Caffe Roma a week after we initially discussed her Yelp and TripAdvisor reviews.

"I just wasn't raised that way," Irene says as we discuss the impact of recent online complaints of her business. "If someone has a problem with how they've been treated, I don't know why they don't come talk to me. Today it seems like some people just want to slam you on review sites." We sit in the back of her busy café as Irene takes a break from running the daily operations. In a small suburban strip mall, today Caffe Roma serves as a meeting place for older Italian Americans, who talk in loud animated discussions.

The café appears to cater to opposite ends of the age spectrum. Several tables in the main area, as well as a narrow area off the main room dubbed "Internet row," are occupied by twenty-somethings with their laptops open, working or watching online videos courtesy of the café's free WiFi. One couple occupies a window table, shoulders hunched and necks hyperextended with chins on their chests as they both text on their smartphones. I wonder if they're texting friends or forgoing verbal communication and texting each other. Irene is gazing over to the telecommuters scattered throughout the main area as we talk about the challenges of online reviews.

There's a Starbucks only three hundred feet from Caffe Roma to the south, and another less than a half mile to the north. Telecommuters abound at both locations, occupying every available table with latte, laptop, smartphone, and other work paraphernalia. The national chain of more than eighteen thousand stores worldwide can easily absorb the cost for creating what Starbucks terms "the third place," or a living room environment where customers can linger, meet friends, or find a public environment to work.

As owner of a small, family-run business, Irene doesn't have the luxury of providing customers with a Starbuck's third place. Several of her one-star reviews are the result of an ongoing battle between café owner and wired cyber-squatters who occupy valuable table space while generating minimal revenue. As noon approaches, the café begins to fill up with lunch patrons who dine on salads, sandwiches, and pasta dishes.

"I can't have tables for four occupied by one guy who buys one cup of coffee in the morning, straight through the lunch rush." Irene recounts a recent incident where during lunch a customer occupied a "four top" while a family of four stood with their food waiting for a table to clear. When Irene politely asked the customer to move to one of the smaller tables to make room for lunch customers, the customer decided to leave.

Several days later, Peter M. posted this two-star review:

> Beware. These people are wifi nazis. I had started to become a regular customer, emphasis on the term "customer." I had been there about 10 times and bought food and drink every time. The last time I was continually harassed by one of the owner/managers to buy something and then asked to leave after about an hour.[1]

Irene can either forgo lunch revenue by accommodating patrons like Peter M. in order to protect her online reputation, or she can ask Peter and his ilk to leave and deal with the negative feedback. Caught in a no-win scenario, Irene is experiencing one of the common problems in the hospitality industry: negotiating the balance between making an emotional connection with a customer and running a profitable business. While Irene is accustomed to providing a high level of service by making each customer feel they're part of an extended family, there are times when certain customers require that Irene cross over into a business mode, like displacing the cyber-squatter despite the potential for negative reviews and lost customers.

In his bestselling book *Predictably Irrational*, Dan Ariely, professor of behavioral economics at Duke University, discusses this phenomenon, which he titles the costs of social norms. According to Ariely, "we live simultaneously in two different worlds—one where social norms prevail, and the other where market norms make the rules."[2] As Ariely discovers, when you try to apply business rules to social relationships, the relationship suffers. Once the line back into business has been crossed, getting that sense of friendship back can be difficult, if not impossible.[3]

In New Haven, Connecticut, Lulu de Carrone, proprietor of Lulu European Coffee House, had noticed that there was a growing discontent between her "laptoppers" and her regular clientele. She also noticed that her café, which she envisioned as a meeting place for friends and conversation, was growing silent as computer users were taking up room and exclusively engaging with their computers. In 2012, Lulu decided to declare her coffeehouse a laptop- and WiFi free-zone. Rather than reading complaints on Yelp, Lulu found that her online reviews grew more positive. Online reviewer Gale Z. writes:

> I love stopping by Lulu's if I have a few spare minutes, am in East Rock, and want to grab a coffee and relax. Lulu is friendly and welcoming and doesn't allow laptops in her cafe, so people actually mingle, and meet, and have interesting conversations, or just savor the coffee and baked goods and look at newspapers, in the cozy seating area or in the sidewalk seating. It's kind of a magical little place, really.[4]

While going sans Internet might not be for every café owner, Lulu's policy represents a paradigm shift for her business. When faced with a dilemma of pleasing two different types of customers, her laptoppers and her social clientele, she returned to her vision of a European coffeehouse where people come to mingle and meet. In the end, Lulu and the café's core clientele are happier.

Irene, however, is still struggling to find that balance between making customers feel at home and having her telecommuting customers take up space in the prime lunchtime hour. According to Ariely,

> If you're a company, my advice is to remember that you can't have it both ways. You can't treat your customers like family one moment and then treat them impersonally—or, even worse, as a nuisance or a competitor—a moment later when this becomes more convenient or profitable. This is not how social relationships work. If you want a

social relationship, go for it, but remember that you have to maintain it under all circumstances.[5]

The proliferation of online sharing and online reviews has raised the bar for service across many industries. Though excellent service is the key to getting the fifth star, going behind that fifth star is about building and maintaining a strong emotional connection with a customer.

I recently sat down at a new neighborhood restaurant with my wife. We were the first diners to eat there on opening day. Our young waiter had clearly been trained to establish a strong emotional connection with his tables. "You guys are our first guests. . . ." In that split second, our waiter's slip revealed the fine line between a business relationship and a social experience. The waiter is still friendly, but now we're guests, as if we're visiting a friend's house for dinner. With that quick change in phrasing, my expectations for service also change.

Now that we're friends of our new neighborhood restaurant, I might feel that normal business rules don't apply. If I want to spend a little more time at my table, I now expect that my new friends would accommodate me. If, in the case of Caffe Roma, I was asked to vacate my table to make way for paying lunch customers, I might feel a little more upset than I would have if we remained in a business, rather than a social, relationship.

The natural inclination for restaurant and small business owners is to push the social/friend boundary with customers as businesses are constantly under fire to differentiate based on service. Larger businesses, like national hotel and retail chains, don't have the same challenge. Their large organizational structure makes true friendship improbable, and attempts by employees to try to manufacture the friendship often feel contrived. Still, some large national chains have excelled at garnering positive reviews while maintaining their business/customer relationship.

Golden Rule 2.0

There is a commonality that runs through London's Hotel 41, Jay's locksmith service, Veo, and other businesses that have garnered five-star reviews—excellent service. However, providing the type of excellent service that wows online reviewers into providing five-star ratings is not as easy as it sounds. To many, the challenge of providing truly excellent service begins with the definition. Jay the locksmith mentioned that along the path to finding the right formula for Lockbusters, an acquaintance who worked for a five-star hotel chain schooled him in the art of service excellence. Jay was fascinated by the amount of attention to detail that went into the execution of five-star service. "There's a certain way of talking, phrases that they use, postures," Jay remembers.

Since most positive online reviews are driven by service, I decided to study a company that is best known for delivering the highest-quality experience for their guests, the Four Seasons hotel chain. While it might seem like providing excellent service across ninety-two hotels in thirty-eight countries would be mind-boggling, every employee's definition of excellent service begins and ends with one specific rule developed by Isadore Sharp, the hotel's founder. In the words of Sharp, "the reason for our success is no secret. It comes down to one single principle that transcends time and geography, religion and culture. It's the Golden Rule—the simple idea that if you treat people well, the way you would like to be treated, they will do the same."[6] I met with the general manager of one of the hotel chain's premier resorts to find out if that's really all it takes.

John O'Sullivan has been employed by Four Seasons since 1995. When I ask how his job has changed since the advent of sites like TripAdvisor, he remarks that the industry really hasn't changed, alluding to the Golden Rule. John still imparts on his staff the necessity to treat each guest the way that they would like to be treated. The one thing that has changed, he mentions, is that with online consumer reviews, guests are armed with an amazing amount of information. Instead of an "us versus them" mentality that many business owners have about online reviews, John acknowledges that "there's a communal ownership of information, and more and more consumers are aware of the agony, and the ecstasy, of online reviews." One huge positive he sees with online reviews is that it's a conversation starter. He goes on to explain that in the past, guests would come and go with good and (occasionally) bad experiences. As the GM, unless a guest had reached out to him or his staff, or he was able to meet that guest during their stay, the guest's assessment of their visit would never make it to his attention. With the increasing acceptance of online reviews, he now has the opportunity to begin a dialogue with all the guests who post about his resort online. John is quick to point out, however, that sites like TripAdvisor are not the be-all and end-all of the hospitality industry; they're merely another tool that guests and hotels have as a way of communicating with each other.

Online Reviews Are One of Many Tools

John makes an excellent point. Keeping on top of social media is so important to the hotel chain that they employ an outside service to notify the Four Seasons staff near real time when his property has been mentioned on a social media channel.

Given the Four Seasons' reputation for excellence in customer service, I ask John what general advice he would give to businesses about approaching online reviews. I've distilled his comments into three main points:

1. Be Where Your Customer Is

It's important that the Four Seasons staff matches the communication habits of its guests. John mentions that in the past "most guests that had questions or requests would end up at the hotel's front desk or concierge desk. Now those same guests might be making requests on Facebook or Twitter." For example, while a guest sits poolside waiting for a drink, they might tweet to the hotel's address that they're waiting for their drinks. With the Four Seasons' obsessive focus on solving their guests' every need, it's of paramount importance that they match their guests' communication patterns, from 140-character tweets to reviews posted on TripAdvisor and Yelp.

2. Embrace Intellectual Curiosity

According to John, intellectual curiosity and a passion for finding mistakes are part of the Four Seasons' staff's DNA. When asked if all the executives embraced participating in online reviews from the beginning, John said that there was little resistance due to that same passion for finding mistakes. When a bad review is posted on a business's profile, the natural reactions for most owners and managers are anger, resentment, and, in some cases, denial. It still seems that most business owners choose to completely ignore negative reviews. That's not the case at the Four Seasons, where reaction to negative feedback on social media is no different from seeing an unhappy guest at one of their hotels when a Four Seasons staff member would check in to see if they could do anything to make that guest happy. To John, a negative review is the same as seeing that unhappy guest, and that intellectual curiosity encourages him to figure out what went wrong. What can the staff do to fix the problem? And, most important, is there something to learn from this negative review that would help improve their business?

3. Apply the Golden Rule

Isadore Sharp's Golden Rule is still the foundation for providing superior service. In the case of reviews, imagine you're a hotel guest who has had a less than optimum experience. Wouldn't you want the business to go out of its way to make things right? Next time you read your negative reviews, imagine yourself in the reviewer's position experiencing what they did. Did you do everything you could to make the situation right? Did you learn from the experience, work toward correcting the problem, and, in the process, improve service?

While applying the Golden Rule would be a great first step for any business owner seeking to improve their customer service, the Four Seasons Golden Rule might need an update given the evolution of the socially connected consumer. Along with the flow of massive amounts of information, the social media age has empowered consumers to express their individuality. The challenge I see with the Four Seasons rule is that it implies that both a guest and a hotel employee will share the same perspective regarding service.

While the Golden Rule still holds in a general sense, treating customers in a way that you would like to be treated is not as clear-cut as it was when Sharp promulgated the rule fifty years ago. Since the inception of the Four Seasons brand, behavior norms and manners have changed, along with the way guests communicate with the staff, one another, and the world. A twenty-one-year-old student and a sixty-five-year-old retiree will have very different views on how they would like to be treated. With the advent of social media, both guests have a bullhorn to broadcast their appreciation or displeasure to anyone who will listen. The Golden Rule seems outdated in a world with such varied consumers.

Our newfound individuality plays out and presents a challenge for business owners and their staff. During a visit to meet

John, I notice a loud hotel guest on his cell phone by the pool. The couple sitting next to the loud talker appear to be on their honeymoon, and they're annoyed by the noisy intrusion. As one of the honeymooners attempts to catch the eye of the pool attendant, it's clear he'd like the attendant to intercede and ask the loud talker to take his call somewhere else. Applying the concept of the Golden Rule, what's the right course of action for the pool attendant? Should he treat the honeymoon couple the way that he would like to be treated by asking the businessman to move, or should he put himself in the position of the businessman? There's a quiet pool a few hundred yards from where the honeymoon couple have staked out their chaise lounges; if they want quiet they could move. This is similar to a café owner who finds herself dealing with a non-revenue-generating customer taking up valuable table space with his laptop computer while a family buying lunch is left standing in the dining area waiting for a table to clear.

While there is no easy answer, online reviews can provide business owners with a valuable source of data to help understand how customers, clients, and guests like to be treated. Scanning negative reviews for your own business as well as your competitors will provide a near-unlimited source of anecdotes of these unfolding dramas. While I could spend countless hours bemoaning the decay of decorum and manners, that would do little to change the way social interactions are changing. However, by studying consumer opinions, you can get closer to understanding your customers and delivering service in line with Golden Rule 2.0: treat others the way that they like to be treated.

In recent years, the advent of daily deals such as Groupon and

Living Social has presented a unique challenge to our new Golden Rule. While we might try to win customers by providing excellent customer service, providing customers with steep discounting can reduce the customer relationship to a commoditized relationship.

The Group Coupon / Online Review Conundrum

Inboxes are inundated with group coupons. Spend ten dollars and get twenty dollars' worth of goods, 50 percent off, 75 percent off. The discounting seems to be interminable, and the recent proliferation of group coupons and steep discounting has put another strain on the friend/business relationship. In what was initially designed as a customer acquisition strategy, many businesses have realized that when offering group coupons to their customers, there's often a resulting decline in their average online review rating. Groupon, founded in November 2008, was the first of many group-discounting sites that offered businesses a new customer acquisition model. Get customers into your business to try your product by offering a social-based coupon. In order for a coupon to become active, a certain number of customers, known as a tipping point, had to buy.

When first introduced, the concept was wildly popular. The businesses offering the deals were inundated with new customers, at times so many that they couldn't take the volume of new customers and buckled under the weight. As businesses struggled to figure out a way to utilize the customer acquisition tool without overloading, an interesting effect was noticed. Whenever a business offered a group coupon, their online star rating, specifically their Yelp average rating, declined. There are several theories as to why this coupon-driven decline in online ratings occurs.

John Byers of Boston University and his colleagues authored a root cause analysis to figure out the cause of the ratings decline by analyzing data sets from Yelp.[7] The potential causes that were tested included an intrinsic decline (that the decline in reviews was completely independent of the coupon offering), that group coupon users are more critical as a group, the assumption that businesses offering group coupons must be in trouble to begin with, that businesses offering group coupons are unprepared to handle the volume of business, and the possibility that businesses treat group coupon users discriminately or more poorly than their average customer.[8]

For those reviews that contained "Groupon" within the Yelp posting, Byers found that Groupon users were less critical than the population, and that Groupon users tended to write longer, more specific critiques of a business than the reviewing population. This is a significant finding, since I have found that those reading reviews tend to give more weight to reviews that are longer.

Byers concluded that one of the primary reasons for the "Groupon effect," or the drop in online review rankings, was bad business practice, as businesses were treating customers presenting group coupons worse than the rest of their customers.

Byers mentions how counterintuitive this finding is, as it doesn't make sense that a business would issue a coupon, providing such a steep discount to get new customers through the door, and then treat those customers poorly.[9]

Outside of Byers' research, there have been several anecdotal reports from business owners noting that Groupon customers have very specific buying behavior, specifically that they are deal seekers. An example of a typical buying behavior would be a group coupon customer who spends the exact dollar amount of the coupon and will likely never return again (unless another group coupon is offered). It's possible that shop owners learned this lesson after they had made the decision to offer a coupon, and thus treated these new customers as a sunk cost as soon as they saw the coupon in their customers' hands.

Another possible explanation that Byers couldn't test for is the difference between how a business owner treats her customers versus how she treats an employee. In a restaurant offering a group coupon this can cause an inherent conflict between customers and staff, as waiters and waitresses earn most of their money in tips. When a business offers a group coupon for 50 percent off (or more), a waitperson's compensation is likely cut in half for a coupon-wielding table.[10]

The Deal Influencer

With the advent of Groupon, its competitors, and the plethora of direct deals from retailers (with large window signs announcing 40, 50, and 60 percent off), the United States has become a deal-seeking society. In segmenting the U.S. population into different types of deal searchers, our data at Experian Marketing Services found that one particular segment, which makes up 18 percent of all U.S. consumers, is of particular interest to any business that thrives on online reviews. The segment, which we call the deal-seeking influentials, are eighteen- to thirty-four-year-olds likely to have young children in the household (this group overlaps with the power reviewers we discussed in chapter 4). This group identifies with the statement "I am obsessed with getting the best possible deal."

Along with deal obsession, this group also thinks of themselves as influencers, believing that their purchases influence what others purchase. According to Experian Marketing Services data, they are adventurous and are 2.3 times more likely than the rest of the population to go online and review their experiences. As discussed with the Groupon effect, certain customers might have a substandard experience when using a social coupon or buying products on sale or clearance, and there's a good chance that one of these shoppers is a deal-seeking influential. Businesses should take special care when catering to these customers, as they are more likely to log on to Yelp from their mobile phones in your store and either tell everyone about the deal they just received or, if crossed, tell their network of the substandard service experienced at your business.

As we drink coffee, I ask Irene of Caffe Roma if she's had any experience with the group coupon effect. She has never offered a group coupon for her coffee shop. While Irene is old school, believing in the concept of face-to-face conversations with her customers versus interacting with them over postings and comments on online review sites, the way consumers are interacting with businesses is changing. While Irene may never need to offer a coupon to get business, the trove of data available in online review postings could provide an invaluable source of competitive intelligence for businesses that make certain business choices. I know that if I were to ask Irene to analyze her reviews, she'd end up focusing on the negative ones, and would likely stop before doing a complete analysis. I offer to take a look at her reviews and come up with my own analysis.

When Irene Is Not There

Irene, along with running a very successful business, is also a mom. She runs the café in the mornings during the week, but by midafternoon, her managers take over as she leaves to pick up her kids from school.

I take the afternoon to write from Irene's café (but I make sure to buy coffee and something to eat as soon as I get there). I'm troubled by the dichotomy of Caffe Roma's reviews. Most are glowing and mention Irene and her miraculous talent for remembering every customer's name after just meeting them once, while others mention shortcomings in the staff and a manager who can be rude at times. Around three o'clock in the afternoon, I notice something. The staff later in the afternoon is a little more lax; there are several tables that haven't been cleared, and the music in the café has changed—it's louder and not the same mix. As I walk out the door I see one of the staff sitting on a back counter checking her cell phone. I doubt that would happen if Irene were here.

When Irene and I meet several weeks later, I've prepared an analysis for her of her own Yelp and TripAdvisor reviews. We talk about the difference in the café when she's not there, and I bring up some negative reviews that clearly paint the picture of things not running as smoothly in the afternoons. I've piqued her interest in monitoring reviews, and Irene declares that she's going to have a staff meeting to talk about them.

10

★ ★ ★ ★ ★

The Future of Reviews

* * * * *

As I exit the W hotel in Union Square, I scan Park Avenue for an available cab; unfortunately, the doorman of the hotel is nowhere to be found. It's now three-thirty and I realize that if I don't get a cab soon I'll be stuck between shift change (when cab drivers notoriously go off duty as they begin their trip home) and the dreaded rush-hour traffic that can turn a thirty-five-minute ride to JFK into a ride that could stretch over an hour. I make the decision to use Uber, one of my new favorite smartphone applications, which provides on-demand Lincoln Town Car service. The app notifies me that my driver is just around the corner, and within three minutes a black car pulls up at the front door of the hotel. I also notice that, according to Uber, Robert, my driver, has a 4.8-star rating.

Robert exits the car and helps me get my luggage into the trunk. I stretch out in the backseat, appreciating the comfort of the limousine compared to a New York City cab's backseat, which can be a very uncomfortable configuration for a six-foot

passenger. Cab and limousine drivers in the city can be fascin-
ating to talk to, and I've found that limo drivers in particular
are usually good barometers for how the economy is doing. As
we leave the tunnel I ask Robert about his experience with
Uber. He tells me that 100 percent of his business comes from
Uber, it keeps him busy, and he's happy with the service.

When I mention his 4.8-star rating and the book I'm working on, Robert becomes concerned and tells me that if his rating
were to fall below 4 stars he'd be kicked off the Uber system. I'm
fascinated by how the service works, and Robert tells me he can
choose from requests that are closest to him, but he also has the
choice to turn down a fare. "Why would you turn down a fare?"
I ask. "We're not the only ones that are reviewed," he replies. For
a minute I'm lost, then it hits me. "Wait, I have an Uber rating?,"
I ask. Robert nods his head. He has nine seconds to decide
whether to reply to my request for a car; if he doesn't answer, or
if he turns me down because my rating isn't high enough, my
request goes on to the next driver. When I get out of his car, the
Uber app automatically pulls up a review page, with a picture of
my driver and five empty stars. Tap on the last star and you've
given the driver a top rating; tapping any star below that results
in a lower rating. The rating system for drivers to rate their ride
is very similar.

I strike up a conversation with another Uber driver who accepted my ride request from San Francisco International. He
doesn't want to be named for fear of reprisals from Uber. My
driver says that he won't accept a ride request from anyone with a
4.6 or below. He seems conflicted about the whole review economy.

From a rider's perspective I applaud the harsh review criteria that Uber imposes on its drivers. In the many rides that I have hailed via my iPhone, I have never had a negative experience. From my driver's perspective it's not always that positive. "People are not always nice," my driver says, and proceeds to tell me about one of his experiences working a late-night shift and accepting a ride request from Uber. Arriving at the fare's location, he realized that the rider wanted him to take six people in his town car. After informing her that he wasn't allowed to take more than four people, words and a one-star review ensued. He was temporarily kicked off the service.

For all the complaints about shill reviews, vendettas, conflicts of interest, and other sources of "noise," reviews still hold the promise of playing a vital function in facilitating transactions. In the case of the seamless digital negotiation that occurred in the three minutes between my request for a driver and taking a seat in Robert's car, a sense of trust was formed on my part knowing that I could trust my driver, and Robert had a sense of security in knowing that he was picking up a fare who had a positive history with other drivers. That same trust provided by reviews is what allowed online marketplaces such as eBay to flourish. After all, without some sense of knowing whom you are dealing with, would you really be willing to enter a transaction blind? The fact that eBay is able to process several million transactions per day is a testament to the importance that reviews play in the completion of online transactions.

Online reviews play a critical role in the marketplace. Significant challenges remain to their viability, primarily the accuracy and reliability of the information relayed via a simple post, but despite all the complaints about the inadequacies of reviews, over the last several years they have benefited both customers and businesses.

Customer Benefits

Transparency

Jay the locksmith's business transparency in what he charges and the services that he delivers was a clear benefit to his business. By putting everything out there, and having the review public verify his transparency, his business and others that have chosen to differentiate based on transparency will bring consumers closer to the ideal of making informed decisions.

Accountability

Along with transparency, businesses are quickly learning that they are becoming increasingly accountable for the quality of their products and services. While in prior decades businesses could be built on brand through advertising, in the review economy, the value of a brand can diminish as it's publicly held accountable for what is put in the marketplace.

Level of Service

What may scare business owners the most about online reviews is that the two benefits of transparency and accountability drive the market toward commoditization. In a marketplace where the consumer has near-perfect information and knows exactly what she will receive in goods and services for the money she spends, the antidote to the pressure that commoditization brings is quality of service. I might just be selling you a head of lettuce at the corner grocery store, but if I can make your purchase more enjoyable by providing a welcoming environment, friendly employees, or an overall more enjoyable experience than what you might have at a large supermarket, my ability to break commoditization increases.

In a perfect world, as businesses race to differentiate based on their level of service, the quality of service rises for everyone. In the review economy great service replaces brand as a differentiator. The nature of reviews is still imperfect, and the concept that everyone wins still feels theoretical. The challenges of reviewer veracity, conflict of interest, competing incentives, and varying perspectives continue to stand in the way of reaching the ideal of a perfectly informed marketplace. The good news is that market inefficiencies are the playground for new innovation. Given the amount of money at stake in improving the marketplace, I am confident that new companies and technologies are poised to bring us closer to a more reliable review-driven marketplace.

Businesses also stand to gain from the growth of online reviews.

Benefits to Business

New Acquisition Channel

In the past, the acquisition of new customers was a function of how much money you had to spend to advertise and develop brand, giving larger companies with big advertising budgets the advantage over smaller businesses. Online reviews represent the first acquisition channel that is merit-based versus cash-based, or, in other words, your acquisition of new customers will come down to how good your products and services are instead of how much money you have to spend on reaching prospective buyers. This business advantage is a discriminate one, benefiting only those businesses that are nimble enough to connect with their customers in a way that drives positive reviews.

As online review platforms improve their ability to reduce the noise of fake reviews, and customers choose which businesses to purchase from based on quality, I can deduce that the net effect will be a decrease in advertising spent across the board.

Feedback Loop

With the reduction of fake reviews comes the advantage of having a feedback loop that helps businesses to better serve their customers by monitoring the sentiment of online reviews. Over time, as more consumers write online reviews, customer satisfaction surveys will become extinct and businesses will use reviews to monitor and incentivize employees to meet the needs of customers and drive business through positive reviews.

In the future not every business will benefit from the growth and refinement of online review platforms. Transparency will have its price for businesses that provide less than excellent products and services, whose owners and employees are punching time clocks rather than obsessing on delivering excellence.

Essentially, online reviews will lead to the business equivalent of evolution's survival of the fittest.

How will the landscape change and what does the future hold for this new channel? Where are online reviews headed, and what innovations can we expect to see in the near future?

Prediction: Google Reviews Become the Dominant Player

Google is the single biggest supplier of traffic to all of the major online review sites. According to Experian Marketing Services data, 82 percent of Yelp's traffic comes from search engines; Google accounts for 60 percent of that traffic, while Yahoo! Search and Bing make up the majority of the remainder. Google also has control of the demand for local information. According to Google, 20 percent of all searches are local.[1] With Google's newly improved business interface, Google Places for Business, business owners will have the capability of tracking and managing review channels along with other marketing functions, like local paid search listings. Although Google's majority of revenue comes from paid search advertising, the appearance of conflict of interest is far less than Yelp's. In 2013, Facebook also augmented its online review capabilities by adding star ratings to its business pages, but Google still has the advantage of controlling supply in the form of consumer searches.

Prediction: Reviews Become (Mostly) Bilateral

In the early days of online reviews, the marketplace and trust created on eBay were driven by the reviews of both buyer and seller. Today there are a number of review-driven businesses that function based on reviews from both parties. As I experienced during my Uber ride to the airport with Robert, the prospect of reviewees reviewing the reviewer adds an interesting dynamic. Airbnb, the San Francisco vacation rental start-up, is another great example of a marketplace that is driven by bilateral reviews. I can't think of a case where reviews become more critical than when renting out a property you own, in some cases your own house.

In June 2011, a property owner and Airbnb renter with the handle "EJ" detailed her horror story of a renter who had ransacked her apartment while she was away on a weeklong business trip.[2] Beyond completely trashing her apartment, the Airbnb renter stole material items and potentially EJ's identity.

> They smashed a hole through a locked closet door, and found the passport, cash, credit card and grandmother's jewelry I had hidden inside. They took my camera, my iPod, an old laptop, and my external backup drive filled with photos, journals . . . my entire life. They found my birth certificate and social security card, which I believe they photocopied—using the printer/copier I kindly left out for my guests' use.[3]

A few days after the incident, Airbnb responded with an apology to EJ as well as instituting a fifty-thousand-dollar guarantee for any damages sustained during an Airbnb stay.[4] While this is a substantial reward, there still must be a great deal of concern when anyone considers opening his or her home to a complete stranger. Perhaps nothing will completely assuage the fear that EJ's experience evokes, but verified reviews must help.

As with the eBay marketplace, bilateral reviews can serve the critical function of providing a sense of trust. In the case of eBay, Airbnb, Uber, and others that provide reviews in both directions, the parties are on equal footing. This concept of reviews for both parties should also be considered within the context of the deep-rooted social norm "The customer is always right." Imagine a restaurant being able to review its diners: "cheap diner, didn't leave a tip"; or a hotel reviewing its guests: "this slob left the room a mess and ate everything in the mini-bar without letting us know when he checked out." Such a free flow of information on both sides of the equation might seem ridiculously far-fetched, but is it?

OpenTable has a VIP status for diners who have made and kept twelve reservations within a year. While providing insight into only one aspect of the quality of a restaurant patron, in today's age of missed dining reservations (in major cities like New York, the percentage of no-shows can reach as high as 20 percent[5]), the knowledge that a potential patron has a track record for keeping his commitment to dine at a restaurant has significant value. OpenTable's VIP program might not appear to be a bilateral review, but when considering that the status is determined via an electronic confirmation from the restaurant that a diner showed up, the feedback loop, at least on reliability, is complete.

Given the social norm of deferring to the customer, it's

unlikely that restaurants will start reviewing the guests who patronize their establishments. Since online reviews didn't provide a forum other than in his own comments section, a restaurant owner in Los Angeles decided to cross the line. Noah Ellis, an owner of Red Medicine, became irate when turning down walk-in customers because no-show diners didn't appear for their appointed reservations. On a busy night in March, Ellis tweeted:

> All the nice guests who wonder why restaurants overbook and they sometimes have to wait for their res should thank people like those below.

The restaurant's Twitter account then fired off a second tweet listing the names of seven parties who didn't show that evening. One user on Twitter responded:

> @redmedicinela if more restaurants did this, people might be more respectful. It's like reverse Yelp.

Not everyone was amused with Red Medicine's no-show "outing." Some customers took to Yelp to fight back. David V. wrote:

> I love your food and eat there at least once a month but I think it is EXTREMELY tasteless of you to shame your customers. Maybe you should stop taking reservations and just do walk-ins only. A lot of very busy restaurants do that. It might keep you from getting SO upset about no shows. I want to come back to your restaurant but I don't know if I will, I don't like all the anger.

While other filtered one-star reviews mirroring David V.'s sentiment began to appear on Yelp, Red Medicine's actions garnered significant press coverage for such an unorthodox tactic, and highlighted the popularity of the restaurant evidenced by its need to turn walk-ins away. I don't suggest that other businesses follow in Red Medicine's footsteps, but this bold move by the L.A. eatery exemplifies the growing frustration that some business owners feel for the asynchronous communication that online reviews facilitate.

Excluding changes in social norms, the best option for business owners is to rate reviews themselves. Many review sites, including Amazon, Yelp, and TripAdvisor, ask visitors to their sites to add quality ratings to reviews by voting on whether a review was "helpful," "useful," "funny," or "cool."

Even if we could solve the challenge of asynchronous information, the problem of perspective still remains. Customers bring their own experiences to an establishment when they choose to review. "It's not really the business that is being reviewed," Mohawk Matt points out, "it's the reviewer's experience that is being reviewed." I'll add a small variation to Matt's insight. It's the customer's perspective of a business that forms the basis for most reviews. If you can get past the phony reviews and vendettas, the problem of perspective is the most vexing for business owners. From McDonald's to The French Laundry, Motel 6 to the Four Seasons, reviews provide businesses with a constant reminder of the adage that you can't please everyone all of the time. The 2.0 ending to that sentence should be "There's an app for that."

To date, the solution to help find perspective is to leverage social networks to provide people you might know based on the assumption that our "friends" have tastes that are similar to our own. By adding insight to what they like, your friends will help you discover things that you like with greater accuracy. The mash-up of social networks manifests itself in two primary ways. First, within review sites there is the opportunity for visitors and reviewers to form their own networks; and second, several review networks have links to Facebook, which allows visitors to see which of their "friends" also likes a particular hotel, restaurant, or other business. TripAdvisor employs this linkage, so when viewing hotel rankings you can see which of your friends have stayed at that hotel.

For finding perspective based on existing networks, the challenge is the manual nature of selecting who to follow, and that the reason you chose to follow a specific reviewer could be simply because you enjoyed their writing style, liked their humor, or agreed with them on one (but not all) aspects of a particular review. For Facebook-linked reviews, there is an apparent problem. Take a look at the number of friends you have within the world's largest social network. It's likely that they are family, friends, work contacts, high school friends, acquaintances, someone you met at a party, or friends of friends (of friends). Now ask yourself how many of these people have the same taste that you do in books, music, coffee, or pizza. You'll soon discover that adding this level of information to online reviews adds little to help provide you with perspective.

Prediction: The Future—Reviews Become Data

The data is there. It exists today. One of the by-products that have emerged from consumers putting so much information on social networks, into search engines, and on review sites is that there is a mountain of behavioral data by which companies could impute perspective. In terms of finding the right perspective in online reviews, it can be done today, as the mentality that you can please everyone forms the foundation for finding and filtering reviews based on perspective.

I often use my wife as an example of the manual process of review perspective through triangulation. Within review sites like TripAdvisor, it's possible to reveal all the properties reviewed by any specific reviewer. Here's where the triangulation comes into play. When preparing for our last trip to Hawaii, Lori first visited TripAdvisor to find the most highly rated hotels on the island of Maui. Lori knew from past experience that not all reviewers share our likes and dislikes in hotel rooms, cost, amenities, on-property dining, etc., so, one by one, she went through the most recent reviews for each property we were considering, studied each reviewer in context of their review history, looking for reviews of properties that we'd already visited, and would then determine if we would have agreed on past properties. The process of manual triangulation in hotel searches can take hours, as most properties now have hundreds of reviews. Wouldn't it be wonderful if there were an automated process to handle this time-consuming task?

As we've seen with user reviews, searching based on the behaviors of "friends" within social networks has limited returns.

What is most exciting about the future is that when search engines and review sites will be able to employ algorithms to use our online behavior and preferences in online criticism and reviews, new doors will open to make reviews more useful. It's not a straight course to get to that end goal, as there are some significant challenges that stand in the way.

One of the biggest objections to mining and utilizing online user behavior is the competing interest of our desire for privacy, specifically in our online lives. With time, however, consumers are balancing those privacy concerns with the benefit of getting better information online. If, as a consumer, you could save hours and truly find the best hotels, books, music, or masseuse based on your past likes and dislikes, how much of your online privacy would you be willing to give up?

Another challenge is the disputed accuracy of reviews, and within that the chief complaint is the problem that many people who write criticism on a business online didn't necessarily visit or buy goods from that business. Over the years, several startups in the review sector have tried to build their businesses on verified reviews, but few have survived.

Prediction: Review Sites Will Be Forced to Ride a Razor's Edge to Solve Conflicts of Interest

Competition solves many problems. There was a time when sites like Yelp and TripAdvisor had a monopoly on the review market. While they are still the biggest players in their market, challenges such as conflicts of interest provide an opportunity for new and reimagined competitors to solve.

Through its Google+ Local search product, Google now provides reviews of businesses that are presented when a searcher executes a local search or when a searcher searches for businesses near a location using Google Maps. While Google is also in the business of selling advertising, ads on Google+ Local are such a small portion of Google's revenue that the chance of a conflict of interest is much lower. Facebook is also poised to enter the review market. In 2013, Facebook added a feature to their business and mobile product sites to enable reviews that compete with Yelp and Google+ Local. Facebook also announced its Graph Search, where users can search for a business type, a music artist, or a book, and limit their search to suggestions that their friends or friends of friends like. Users will even be able to limit their search to a single individual. I can type "restaurants that Natalya Rybicka likes in New York" to get to very specific friend-trusted recommendations. Since Facebook made the announcement, Yelp's CFO publicly signaled that Yelp was interested in partnering with the social network giant.[6]

Prediction: Algorithms Will Advance as Fake Review Posters Become More Sophisticated

Review sites can bet that scammers, "reputation businesses," and unscrupulous owners will continue to pen fake reviews. We can expect to see additional resources devoted to improving algorithms to spot these fraudulent reviews. Along with today's technology of looking at IP addresses and geographic locations, additional innovation in linguistic-based filtering should be expected. Since the core value of review sites revolves around accurate, trusted reviews, the imperative of weeding out phony reviews is at the top of the list.

Along with existing competitors and new algorithms, new competitors can expect to enter the marketplace with a fresh view on how to crack the review economy.

Thinking back to my conversations with Irene and Misti, both business owners were troubled by the same thing, that this change in technology is eroding some of our social fiber. When someone had problems with a business in the past, the only recourse they had was to talk to the owner or manager about their problem. Now we have enabled consumers to skip that step and tell the world about a breakdown in service, or about a product that didn't work in the way that they were expecting. While there does seem to be some erosion in how we treat one another, relying on anonymity and textual attacks to make our point rather than a face-to-face discussion to resolve a problem, I also remember my conversations with Mohawk Matt and Jay the locksmith. Both gentlemen have experienced the exact same changes in the way consumers interact with their businesses via review sites, but both Matt and Jay have chosen to embrace the change rather than deride it. I can honestly say that I see both sides. I understand how frustrating it can be for the business owner when someone decides to vent, often for reasons beyond their control.

One thing I think both sides will agree on is that with the

advent of online reviews, there is a wealth of data and insight that can help business owners keep tabs on how customers are changing, their challenges, and their preferences. I also think everyone would agree that there is an amazing opportunity in the new landscape for businesses to raise their level of service now that they are armed with what they know about customers. The businesses that will win are those that know their end point, embrace transparency, and go the extra mile to earn their fifth star.

ACKNOWLEDGMENTS

In a world full of critics, I am very fortunate to be surrounded by friends and colleagues who have made this book possible. Before I let you go, I have a few reviews of my own that I'd like to post.

★ ★ ★ ★ ★

Melissa Flashman—Trident Media Group

Mel is the publishing whisperer, an amazing agent and friend who saw the potential in writing a book about online reviews. There's a process that happens between author and agent when a book idea moves from proposal to contract to finished work; Mel was there for every step with spot-on advice. If I could give her an extra star I would.

★ ★ ★ ★ ★

Niki Papadopoulos and Penguin Portfolio

As the editor behind this book, Niki had the challenging task of functioning as my chief critic, and I couldn't have asked for a better one. I'm very fortunate to have her and the Penguin Portfolio team in my corner.

Acknowledgments

A special thanks to Adrian Zackheim for helping me frame this idea. One thirty-minute meeting with Adrian at the very beginning of the writing process was indispensible. If I could bottle and sell Adrian's form of constructive criticism I'd be a billionaire.

Thanks to Kary Perez for her help during the editing process, the production team for all their work behind the scenes, to Will Weisser for marketing expertise, and Justin Hargett for publicity.

★ ★ ★ ★ ★

My work colleagues

Thanks to the folks at Experian and Experian Marketing Services, Don Robert, Chris Callero, Mike DeVico, Matt Seeley, and Ashley Johnston for encouraging me to write this book. If there was a Yelp for executive teams this group would surely rank #1. Five stars to gurus Bill Schneider and John Fetto who helped me navigate our big data for insights on consumer reviews.

Thanks also to the #1 ranked Experian PR team; Gerry Tschopp, Scott Anderson, Matt Tatham, and Suzanne Blackburn, and my friends on the EMS marketing team Pamela Robertson, for driving me to develop more content and Natalia Rybicka, our very own events whisperer.

★ ★ ★ ★ ★

AirPR

I've been fortunate to serve on the advisory board of AirPR while I was writing this book, and at times I'm not sure who's advising whom. Thanks to Sharam Fouladgar-Mercer and Rebekah Iliff for your innovative ideas in getting the word out. You both are the future of PR.

⭐ ⭐ ⭐ ⭐ ⭐

Friends

Thanks to my friend Jonathan Freedman for being my sounding board; I'm very fortunate to have such a brilliant writing friend. Thanks also to my Saturday biking group, the Roosters; many of my light-bulb moments came to me during our weekly rides through San Mateo, Woodside, and Portola Valley.

⭐ ⭐ ⭐ ⭐ ⭐

Family

I'm very fortunate to have such a supportive family. Thanks to my parents, Martin and Sheila Tancer, for always encouraging me to pursue my dreams.

And thanks to the most important critic of all, my beautiful wife, Lori, for being my support, cheerleader, and best friend. Criticism can have many motivations; Lori's criticism is motivated purely by love and was instrumental in making this book happen. There aren't enough stars in the universe to express how fortunate I am to have her by my side.

NOTES

CHAPTER 1: THE REVIEW REVOLUTION—WHEN
EVERYTHING IS REVIEWABLE

1. Sucharita Mulpuru, Forrester Research, "The Purchase Path of Online Buyers in 2012," http://www.forrester.com/The+Purchase +Path+Of+Online+Buyers+In+2012/fulltext/-/E-RES82001.
2. Zaraida Diaz, YouGov, "21% of Americans Who Have Left Reviews, Reviewed Products without Buying or Trying Them," January 22, 2014, http://research.yougov.com/news/2014/01/22/21 -americans-have-reviewed-products-and-services-t/.
3. TripAdvisor Fact Sheet, http://www.tripadvisor.com/PressCenter -c4-Fact_Sheet.html.
4. Jefferson Graham, "'Yelpers' Review Local Businesses," *USA Today*, June 12, 2007.
5. Yelp.com, "10 Things You Should Know About Yelp" (captured 3/6/14), http://www.yelp.com/about.
6. Toni Anicic, "Customer Reviews and Their Influence on Conversion Rate and Search Engine CTR," August 2, 2001, http://inchoo .net/ecommerce/customer-reviews-and-their-influence-on-conversion -rate-and-search-engine-ctr/.
7. Vikki Morgan, eConsultancy, January 10, 2012, http://econsultancy .com/blog/8638-bad-reviews-improve-conversion-by-67.
8. That's Biz, "Restaurant Owners Think Online Review Sites Are Bad for Business," August 1, 2013, http://www.prweb.com/releases/ 2013/8/prweb10984809.htm.

9. Michael Luca, "Reviews, Reputation and Revenue: The Case of Yelp.com" (working paper, Harvard Business School, September 16, 2011).

10. Michael Anderson and Jeremy Magruder, "Learning from the Crowd: Regression Discontinuity Estimates of the Effects of an Online Review Database," *Economic Journal*, October 5, 2011.

11. Google/Keller Fay Group, "Word of Mouth and the Internet" (study, June 2011) Harvard Business School, November 8, 2013.

CHAPTER 2: WHY BUSINESSES HATE REVIEWS

1. Max Chafkin, "You've Been Yelped," *Inc.*, February 2010, http://www.inc.com/magazine/20100201/youve-been-yelped.html.

2. Freedom of Information Act request by Robert Delaware to the Federal Trade Commission of the United States of America, filed on August 3, 2012, and fulfilled on May 15, 2013, case reference number 39771856.

3. Ibid.

4. FTC response to Freedom of Information Act request.

5. Ibid., case reference number 20400835.

6. Ibid., case reference number 29967104.

7. Michael Luca and Georgios Zervas, "Fake It Till You Make It: Reputation, Competition, and Yelp Review Fraud" (working paper, September 2013).

8. http://sf.eater.com/archives/2013/08/19/groupon_rep_threatens_sauces_owner_with_yelp_army.php.

9. Luca, "Reviews, Reputation and Revenue."

10. Ibid.

11. Danny King, "Cornell Study Links Hotel Reviews and Room Revenue," *Travel Weekly*, November 29, 2012.

12. Mary Pilon, "A Fake Amazon Reviewer Confesses," *Wall Street Journal*, July 9, 2009.

13. http://tripadvisor-reviewers.com/how-it-works/.

14. http://techcrunch.com/2009/01/18/belkin-replies-to-mechanical-turk-shilling/.

15. Arlen Parsa, "Belkin's Development Rep is Hiring People to Write Fake Positive Amazon Reviews," https://web.archive.org/web/20131210135350/http://www.thedailybackground.com/2009/01/16/ex

clusive-belkins-development-rep-is-hiring-people-to-write-fake
-positive-amazon-reviews/.

16. Angus Loten, "Hoping to Fix Bad Reviews? Not So Fast," *Wall Street Journal*, August 6, 2012, http://online.wsj.com/news/articles /SB10000872396390444840104577548982072928526.

17. David Streitfeld, "The Best Book Reviews Money Can Buy," *New York Times*, August 25, 2012.

18. Loten, "Hoping to Fix Bad Reviews?"

19. Kim Severson, "Yelp Them, They'll Help You," *New York Times Blog*, August 31, 2009, http://dinersjournal.blogs.nytimes.com /2009/08/31/yelp-them-theyll-help-you/.

20. Andrew Stephen, "Believe It or Not: Online User Reviews," *Faculty Blog*, University of Pittsburgh, October 7, 2013, http://www .katz.pitt.edu/facultyblog/?p=145.

21. David Streitfeild, "Buy Reviews on Yelp, Get Black Mark," *New York Times*, October 18, 2012.

22. Data set available by request: http://myleott.com/op_spam.

23. Myle Ott, Yejin Choi, Claire Cardie, and Jeffrey Hancock, "Finding Deceptive Opinion Spam by Any Stretch of the Imagination" (*Proceedings of the 49th Annual Meeting of the Association for Computational Linguistics*, June 19, 2011, 309–19).

24. Ibid., 312.

25. Ibid., 311.

26. Ibid., 313.

27. Carlyle Adler, "The Man Behind the VC Slagfest at TheFunded .com Reveals Himself to Wired," *Wired*, November 15, 2007.

28. John Tozzi, "Obama's Pizza Stop Creates Least Helpful Yelp Profile Ever," *Bloomberg Businessweek*, September 11, 2012.

29. Diaz, "21% of Americans," January 2014.

CHAPTER 3: BAD REVIEWS HAPPEN

1. Amazon reviews of *Click: What Millions of People Are Doing Online and Why It Matters*, http://www.amazon.com/Click-Millions-People-Online-Matters/product-reviews/1401323049/ref=cm_cr _pr_hist_2?filterBy=addTwoStar&showViewpoints=0&sortBy =bySubmissionDateDescending.

2. Anthony Bourdain, *No Reservations*, season 1, episode 7, October 17, 2005.
3. TripAdvisor reviews of The French Laundry, August 26, 2009, http://www.tripadvisor.com/Restaurant_Review-g33300 -d493634-Reviews-or10-The_French_Laundry-Yountville_ Napa_Valley_California.html#REVIEWS.
4. Mikaela Conley, "Dentist Threatens to Sue Patient for Negative Yelp Review," ABC News, December 1, 2011.
5. Ibid.
6. "I-Team: Boston Pizza Store Scam?" WBZ-TV, November 17, 2010.

CHAPTER 4: WHO WRITES REVIEWS

1. http://www.yelp.com/faq.
2. Victoria Yue, "Do Asian Americans Yelp Like Crazy?" *Hyphen*, March 31, 2011, http://www.hyphenmagazine.com/blog/archive /2011/03/do-asian-americans-yelp-crazy.
3. Ibid.
4. Reineke Reitsma, *Forrester Blog*, February 15, 2013, http://blogs .forrester.com/reineke_reitsma/13-02-15-the_data_digest _consumer_ratings_and_reviews.
5. Edward F. McQuarrie, Shelby H. McIntyre, and Ravi Shanmugam, "What Motivates Consumers to Produce Online Reviews? Solidarity, Status, and the Soapbox Effect," Social Science Research Network, February 1, 2013, http://ssrn.com/abstract=2210707.
6. Ibid., 13.
7. Edward F. McQuarrie, Shelby H. McIntyre, and Ravi Shanmugam, "What Factors Sustain the Production of Online Reviews? Role of Community Feedback and Differences in Individual Motivation," Social Science Research Network, November 22, 2013, http://ssrn.com/abstract=2358565.
8. Rebecca L.'s restaurant review, http://www.yelp.com/biz/garden -korean-cuisine-federal-way?hrid:IxfzO7zaIOU9UOAgLSek-Q.
9. McQuarrie, "What Factors Sustain the Production of Online Reviews?"

CHAPTER 5: HOW REVIEWS, EVEN BAD ONES, ARE GOOD FOR YOU

1. Heather Somerville, "Popular Salad Buffet Fresh Choice Goes Dark," *San Jose Mercury News*, December 14, 2012.
2. Luca, "Reviews, Reputation and Revenue."
3. Experian Mosaic 2011 geodemographic segmentation.
4. "Bad Reviews Are Good for Business: The Power of Negative Reviews," Reevoo (white paper, no date).
5. Ibid.
6. Panagiotis Ipeirotis, "Big Data, Stupid Decisions" (presentation, Strata Jumpstart 2011, September 19, 2011).
7. Ibid.
8. Ibid.
9. Ibid.
10. Jennifer Bergen, "Zappos Using Amazon Mechanical Turk Since 2009 to Proofread Product Reviews," Geek.com, May 2, 2011, http://www.geek.com/news/zappos-using-amazon-mechanical -turk-since-2009-to-proofread-product-reviews-1351533/.
11. Jonah Berger, Alan T. Sorensen, and Scott J. Rasmussen, "Positive Effects of Negative Publicity: When Negative Reviews Increase Sales," *Marketing Science* 29, no. 5 (September–October 2010): 815.
12. Ibid., 819.
13. Brad Stone, *The Everything Store: Jeff Bezos and the Age of Amazon* (Boston: Little, Brown, 2013), 52.
14. "Bad Reviews Are Good for Business," Revoo.
15. "Bazaarvoice and iPerceptions Team with CompUSA to Analyze Shoppers' Use of Ratings and Reviews," 2006, available at http:// www.businesswire.com/news/home/20061016005539/en/Bazaar voice-iPerceptions-Team-CompUSA-Analyze-Shoppers-Ratings# .U7zfGvldV8E.

CHAPTER 7: DEALING WITH REVIEWS: AFTER THE FACT

1. Bob Krummert, "How to Turn the Tables on Yelp," *Restaurant Hospitality*, November 28, 2012.

2. Kathleen Erickson, "Word of Mouth Marketing," *Agri Marketing*, July–August 2005.
3. Matteo de Angelis, "On Braggarts and Gossips: A Self-Enhancement Account of Word-of-Mouth Generation and Transmission," *Journal of Marketing Research* 49 (August 2012): 552.
4. Ibid., 553.
5. http://www.yelp.com/faq.
6. David Evans, Jill Oviatt, Jordan Slaymaker, et al., "An Experimental Study of How Restaurant-Owners' Responses to Negative Reviews Affect Readers' Intention to Visit," *Four Peaks Review* 2 (June 2012): 1–12.

CHAPTER 8: DEALING WITH REVIEWS PREEMPTIVELY

1. Sarah Moore, "Some Things Are Better Left Unsaid: How Word of Mouth Influences the Storyteller," *Journal of Consumer Research* (April 2012): 1140–54.

CHAPTER 9: BUSINESS AMONG "FRIENDS"

1. Peter M.'s restaurant review, http://www.yelp.com/biz/caffe-roma-coffee-roasting-millbrae?hrid=A0eWd7xXa5nhP_KkJqVpqw.
2. Dan Ariely, *Predictably Irrational: The Hidden Forces That Shape Our Decisions*, rev. and expanded ed. (New York: HarperCollins, 2009), 76.
3. Ibid., 84.
4. Gale Z.'s restaurant review, http://www.yelp.com/biz/lulu-european-coffee-house-new-haven?hrid=i3IFJbCyJannezExk-YCpw.
5. Ariely, *Predictably Irrational*, 87.
6. Four Seasons Web site, http://www.fourseasons.com/about_four_seasons/isadore-sharp/ (captured 7/9/14).
7. John Byers, Michael Mitzenmacher, and Georgios Zervas, "The Groupon Effect on Yelp Ratings: A Root Cause Analysis," *Proceedings of the 13th ACM Conference on Electronic Commerce*, 2012.
8. Ibid., 253.
9. Ibid., 264.
10. While it's customary when using a coupon to tip waitstaff on the amount prior to the discount, it's probable that some diners utilizing coupons don't abide by that custom.

CHAPTER 10 : THE FUTURE OF REVIEWS

1. Marissa Mayer (speech at TechCrunch Disrupt, New York City, May 25, 2011).
2. "Violated: A Traveler's Lost Faith, a Difficult Lesson Learned," *Around the World and Back Again*, June 29, 2011, http://ejround theworld.blogspot.com/2011/06/violated-travelers-lost-faith -difficult.html.
3. Ibid.
4. Ibid.
5. Sumathi Reddy, "Knives Are Out for No-Show Diners," *Wall Street Journal*, March 14, 2012, http://online.wsj.com/news/articles/SB10 00142405270230453790457727944088618260.
6. Chandni Doulatramani, "Yelp Open to Partnering with Facebook's Rival Offering: CFO," Reuters, May 31, 2013, http://www .reuters.com/article/2013/05/31/net-us-yelp-interview-idUSBRE94 U1AC 20130531.

INDEX

Index

Index

Index